The Forgotten Survivors of Gun Violence

"Nearly 40,000 people die from gun violence in the US every year. This uniquely American crisis leaves no community untouched—but it doesn't have to be this way"—Gabrielle Giffords.

The Forgotten Survivors of Gun Violence collects 20 personal essays of survivors' visible and invisible wounds from school shootings, attempted suicide by firearm, mass shootings, gang violence, and domestic violence. Their stories remind us that these traumatic experiences are not exclusive to combat soldiers but, more notably, suffered by ordinary people during modern life. With this collection, editors Loren Kleinman, Shavaun Scott, Sandy Phillips and Lonnie Phillips expose the true lifecycle of a bullet and the trauma left in its wake. Through personal narratives and select personal photos, the wounded tell a story that's forgotten when the cameras go away. This collection will be of interest to first responders, officers, therapists, medical practitioners, and educators.

Loren Kleinman's coverage of gun violence appeared in the *Independent, New York Magazine* (The Cut), *The Rumpus, The New York Daily News*, and more. She is the co-editor of *If I Don't Make It, I Love You: Survivors in the Aftermath of School Shootings* (2019). She is the editor of the anthology *Indie Authors Naked* and the co-edited collection with Amye Archer *My Body, My Words*, which Bustle named one of the "11 New Feminist Books That Could Totally Change Your Year." Her short film, *Suffering Is the Easy Part*, directed and produced by Jaime Ekkens, is distributed by Seed&Spark and Docademia.

Shavaun Scott has been a psychotherapist and writer since 1991 and has worked with thousands of clients who have been victims or perpetrators of violence. She is particularly interested in trauma recovery and violence prevention and enjoys sharing stories of uncommon bravery and unconventional paths. She practices in both Oregon and California.

Sandy Phillips and Lonnie Phillips founded the organization Survivors Empowered after the slaughter of their daughter, Jessica Redfield Ghawi, and 11 others in the Aurora Colorado Theater Mass Shooting in 2012.

Their original non-profit, Jessi's Message, has grown into Survivors Empowered—a national organization created By Survivors, For Survivors, Empowering Survivors. Sandy and Lonnie's story appeared in the documentary *Under the Gun* by Katie Couric and was featured in Lisa Ling's *This is Life* on CNN. They've also been highlighted by media such as *This American Life*, Anderson Cooper, *60 Minutes*, and more.

The Forgotten Survivors of Gun Violence

Wounded

Edited by Loren Kleinman, Shavaun Scott, Sandy Phillips and Lonnie Phillips

LONDON AND NEW YORK

Cover image: © Getty Images

First published 2023
by Routledge
4 Park Square, Milton Park, Abingdon, Oxon OX14 4RN

and by Routledge
605 Third Avenue, New York, NY 10158

Routledge is an imprint of the Taylor & Francis Group, an informa business

British Library Cataloguing-in-Publication Data
A catalogue record for this book is available from the British Library

Library of Congress Cataloging-in-Publication Data
Names: Kleinman, Loren, editor. | Scott, Shavaun, editor. |
Phillips, Sandy (Sandy Anglin), editor. | Phillips, Lonnie, editor.
Title: The forgotten survivors of gun violence: wounded / edited by
Loren Kleinman, Shavaun Scott, Sandy Phillips, Lonnie Phillips.
Description: Abingdon, Oxon; New York, NY: Routledge, 2022. |
Includes bibliographical references and index.
Identifiers: LCCN 2022056459 (print) | LCCN 2022056460 (ebook) |
ISBN 9781032436241 (hardback) | ISBN 9781032436234 (paperback) |
ISBN 9781003368137 (ebook)
Subjects: LCSH: Victims of violent crimes–Psychology. | Victims of violent
crimes–Services for. | Firearms–Social aspects. | Firearms and crime.
Classification: LCC HV6250.25 (print) | LCC HV6250.25 (ebook) |
DDC 362.88–dc23/eng/20221128
LC record available at https://lccn.loc.gov/2022056459
LC ebook record available at https://lccn.loc.gov/2022056460

ISBN: 978-1-032-43624-1 (hbk)
ISBN: 978-1-032-43623-4 (pbk)
ISBN: 978-1-003-36813-7 (ebk)

DOI: 10.4324/9781003368137

Typeset in Bembo
by Newgen Publishing UK

In 2012 our world as we knew it imploded when our only daughter, Jessi, was murdered in the Aurora Colorado Movie Theater Massacre. Had Jessi survived the six bullets that took her life, she would have lived in a vegetative state. Alive... but not living.

Three years later, the killer's trial began, and we pledged that we would be there every day of the trial to represent her and the others affected by the tragedy. During that time, we witnessed the trauma of those affected psychologically and physically.

The wounded in America are always the afterthought of the media and are too often forgotten, but their physical and emotional pain continues. Their lives are forever changed, and they carry scars to remind them of the before and after. Their stories tore at our hearts, and we vowed to honor them in all we do.

This book is dedicated to their grit and spirit to move forward and often create a life which inspires others and pushes them to greatness. It's also dedicated to our Jessi. We honor her spirit and her short life in all we do each day.

Sandy and Lonnie Phillips

Contents

Figures

Foreword: Before and After

Gabby Giffords

Former Congresswoman Gabrielle Giffords is the co-founder of Giffords, an organization dedicated to saving lives from gun violence.

Every person who lives with the trauma of a gunshot wound has a before and an after.

It's hard not to compare the innocence and ease of our "before"—our limitations and challenges at the time that seem small in retrospect, hopes, and dreams that seemed just within our grasp—with the gritty reality of our "afters."

Before, I didn't give walking or talking a second thought. These days, 11 years after I was shot, I still fight for every step and every word.

My path to recovery has been long and winding, full of seemingly insurmountable obstacles and moments of grace and joy. In my "after," I jumped out of a plane. I'm relearning Spanish and the French horn. I ride my bike every day, and recently celebrated my Bat Mitzvah. I burst into song spontaneously.

As Leonard Cohen famously wrote, there are cracks in the darkness, and that's where light gets through. Patience Murray, whose story is shared in these pages, was shot at Pulse Nightclub in 2016. On the worst day of her life, she connected with a man whose sister was murdered that night. They leaned on each other to process their shared trauma and bonded over their love for the Philadelphia Eagles. Today, they're married.

Like Patience, I haven't been on this journey alone. This book showcases so many powerful stories of resilience, perseverance, and courage that I hope make you feel less alone, too.

I lost so much on January 8, 2011, but I didn't lose my life. Six people did, including one of my staffers and a nine-year-old girl. I think about what was taken from their families and communities every day.

Every year, 40,000 people die from gun violence in this country. To honor them and the tens of thousands of other people who are shot and survived, I've dedicated my life to ending the gun violence epidemic.

"People are numb to gun violence in America," writes Alayna Buhr, who was shot while having a night out with her best friends in Dayton, Ohio, in 2019. "It's easier to accept platitudes than to remain angry and worried. The longer people believe gun violence is *just part of life*, the longer it will be a problem."

Storytelling is one the most important tools we have for combatting this numbness. Stories like those in this collection, where survivors bear physical and emotional wounds for all to see, dare us not to look away. If we view this crisis only in statistics, we will forget the human toll of gun violence. We can't let that happen.

I'm so grateful to Sandy, Lonnie, Loren, and Shavaun for creating this collection, and I'm thankful to the survivors who bravely agreed to share their stories in the hopes that something might change: a mind. A heart. A law.

Together, we can build a future free from gun violence. I won't back down until we do.

Acknowledgments

The editors of this book would like to thank the following people for making *The Forgotten Survivors of Gun Violence: Wounded* possible:

- A HUGE THANK YOU to our volunteer copy-editing team Lorna Partington Walsh, Jo Hinton, Liz Kresse Driscoll and Ali Tarbox Saperstein. Lorna and team, we couldn't have done this curation without you and your expertise. Not only are you and your team incredibly empathetic, sensitive and kind, your advice, feedback, and second reads and edits offered another angle to the stories and analysis that made this book whole. We are forever grateful for your dedication and your willingness to help.
- Angela Schellenberg, trauma therapist specializing in grief/loss, resilience. Thank you for connecting us with Shavaun Scott and for your support and generosity. We are all so thankful for your guidance and help.
- Gabby Giffords and the Giffords organization, https://giffords.org/.
- Maxwell Sinsheimer, Sinsheimer Agency.
- Julie Ganz, editor, Skyhorse.
- Amye Archer, co-editor, *If I Don't Make It, I Love You: Survivors in the Aftermath of School Shootings*, https://tinyurl.com/ifidontmakeit.
- Alana Wise, who covers race and identity for NPR's National Desk.
- Cherri Greg, host, WHYY-FM 90.9.
- Gregory Jackson Jr., gun violence survivor and activist, executive director, Community Justice Action Fund, www.cjactionfund.org/.

Editors' Introduction

Loren Kleinman with co-editors Shavaun Scott,
Sandy Phillips, and Lonnie Phillips

> *The toll of America's gun violence epidemic is usually measured in lives lost—more*
> *than 35,000 each year. Ignored, almost completely, are the many more people who are*
> *shot every year, and survive.*
>
> —"Shot and Forgotten," *The Trace,* www.thetrace.org

In the months after co-editing *If I Don't Make It, I Love You: Survivors in the Aftermath of School Shootings,* a collection of 60 narratives covering over 50 years of school shootings in America, Sandy Phillips and Lonnie Phillips, founders of Survivors Empowered, a nonprofit offering support resources to gun violence survivors, asked if I would co-curate a book about the people often forgotten in the aftermath of gun violence: the wounded.

Sandy and Lonnie's daughter, Jessica (Jessi) Redfield Ghawi, was shot and killed on July 20, 2012, in a mass shooting inside a Century 16 movie theater in Aurora, Colorado, during a midnight screening of *The Dark Knight Rises.* Jessi survived the Eaton Centre shooting in Toronto that occurred a month before the Aurora shooting but was among the 12 fatalities on July 20, with 58 others wounded. The aftermath of the shooting was a widening circle of pain inflicted on her family, friends, police, medical first responders, and others. This pain, though, is often not given a second thought after the cameras leave the scene. Those who died were no longer, but those wounded still had their lives to live. However, it is not that simple.

The Forgotten Survivors of Gun Violence: Wounded collects 20 personal essays about the visible and invisible wounds survivors are left with, from armed assault to domestic violence to mass shootings. With almost 40,000 people dying from gun violence in the US annually, this uniquely American crisis leaves no community intact (Giffords Organization). This collection of personal narratives and photos is a reminder that traumatic experiences are not exclusive to combat soldiers but, more notably, suffered by ordinary civilians during modern life, who are often forgotten victims. The following essays expose the lifecycle of a bullet and the trauma left in its wake.

Being wounded is an experience that may never make sense to the survivor. Each survivor has their own ways of coping following the event, often

DOI: 10.4324/9781003368137-1

using a combination of emotional and physical therapy, financial planning, and familial support. However, co-editor and psychotherapist Shavaun Scott describes this wound-lasting lifecycle as nonlinear: "It is in our nature to desire a comprehensible linear narrative about our lives, with clear cause and effect to explain the events that occur." However, that clear line is often blurred when survivors face a deluge of difficulty in the aftermath of inflicted gunshot wounds, such as financial distress, multiple surgeries, and PTSD.

Since many shootings happen randomly, those left in its path often wonder how they will stay safe. Moreover, with the increase in mass shootings in recent decades, just the sound of a car backfiring or a firework cracking across the sky can frighten us. We habitually look for easy access to exits at concert halls. We scan the crowd in shopping malls, grocery stores, and churches for suspicious-looking people who might be armed. Anxiety disorders in the general population are increasing dramatically, and mass shootings are one reason for this.

Though most of us will never experience a mass shooting directly, we are all indirectly affected every time one occurs. Mass shootings have changed how we move through the world and caused collective reverberations of trauma in our society. Throughout this collection, we honor those who have watched loved ones die or those who have gone through the excruciating work of healing from gunshot wounds—not just a scar but a drastic change in their quality of life. Many wounded survivors transition from a completely mobile lifestyle to dependence on wheelchairs and breathing machines, like survivors Kevin Neary and Margaret Long, or prosthetics, like Joshua Nowlan. Some struggle to stay financially afloat, managing what seems like incessant surgeries, like Carolyn Tuft and Patience Murray. Sadly, the list of those living with the aftereffects of visible and invisible gunshot wounds continues far beyond these pages.

While some wounds might heal, many survivors write of their ever-evolving and complicated recoveries, including the financial burden of injuries and loss. Some contributors also had difficulty writing their narratives because of physical impairments, such as lead poisoning flare-ups, nerve damage, and amputation. These injuries have had lasting effects on the survivors featured in this book, leaving some to struggle with medical debts and others requiring long-term unemployment and disability benefits. While we see advocacy playing a significant role in shootings, these survivors have been managing the pain of physical wounds, often disconnecting or isolating them from participating in such advocacy.

We hope this book will serve as the go-to resource for a growing activist population that wants to eradicate gun violence and its horrific aftermath. Since the shooting at Marjory Stoneman Douglas High School in Parkland, Florida, on February 14, 2018, activism around gun control and safer schools has increased, and activist organizations have seen an enormous uptick in membership. According to *Forbes Magazine*, in an article written only one month after Parkland, Moms Demand Action reported 75,000 new volunteers; the Brady Campaign to Prevent Gun Violence started three new chapters and has seen an increase in donations; and Giffords, the organization run by the former Congresswoman Gabrielle Giffords, noted that 43,000 people had donated $1.2 million to end gun violence.

In addition to surging memberships and increasing donations for existing activist groups, Parkland gave rise to several advocacy groups, including #NeverAgain, and the organization responsible for March for Our Lives (MFOL). The march held on March 24, 2018, in Washington, DC, drew an estimated 800,000 people and broke attendance records. Furthermore, research by Dana R. Fisher, professor of sociology at the University of Maryland, found that 27% of attendees had never marched before. MFOL continues to grow, and the founders have embarked on a cross-country tour. Additionally, Change the Ref, Orange Ribbons for Jaime, and Americans for CLASS have all been formed in the wake of the shooting and collectively have over 100,000 followers on Twitter and Instagram.

Americans may be divided on what to do about these shootings, but one thing is clear: we are all finally paying attention. Furthermore, with the growing occurrence of shootings comes widespread urgency for a solution. According to the 2020 Gallup Poll Social Series, most Americans "[more] generally, 57% say that the laws covering the sale of firearms should be made more strict." More and more people are heeding the call for a solution. This book will be a companion to those working hard to understand the widespread devastation in communities affected by gun violence—a community emergency with no one remaining untouched.

Nevertheless, activists are not the only audience that will connect with these survivor stories. Medical and mental health practitioners and academics rely on first-person narratives to contextualize school shootings. For example, in their book *Telling Stories*, professors Mary Jo Maynes, Jennifer L. Pierce, and Barbara Laslett argue that personal narratives— autobiographies, oral histories, life history interviews, and memoirs—are an essential research tool for understanding the relationship between people and their societies. Academics will rely on the authenticity of the first-person point of view to inform and enhance their research and lessons on the topic of school shootings in America.

Moreover, with the publishing of *If I Don't Make It, I Love You: Survivors in the Aftermath of School Shootings*, covering over 50 years of shootings in America, it is clear that readers, academics, and practitioners are committed to reading and connecting with a new generation of primary accounts from wounded survivors of gun violence.

Survivor communities are ready to tell their stories and to hear the stories of others. Since Parkland, we have seen an uptick in survivors coming forward in various media outlets such as *VICE*, *Teen Vogue*, and the *New York Times*. However, some survivors are still media-wary. In seeking contributors for this project, we (the editors) spoke personally with over 50 individuals who have survived attempted suicide, mass shootings, and domestic violence.

More than half of them only agreed to participate because they considered this project to be apart from the news media—a sentiment expressed repeatedly.

There is no "getting over" this kind of loss. No therapeutic template helps someone "move on" after a multilayered heartbreak. There will be no formula for "back to normal," despite the hundreds of books written on the topic. Many survivors of catastrophic loss describe *growing around the grief* that becomes a part of them *but never growing out of it*.

Many find advocacy work a meaningful part of their journey. The best way we can support survivors is to be present with them, listen, attune to their feelings, and never judge their reactions to their experiences. It is normal to strive to understand catastrophic trauma and, as one survivor says, "in the absence of understanding, to make meaning." Nevertheless, by sharing their stories, hope emerges—survivors remake their place in the world and retaliate against the boundary their suffering has imposed on them.

Content guidance: This book explores criminology aspects related to gun violence survivors, specifically the wounds they've endured at the time of the shooting and also visual aspects of their recovery. This book contains scenes that may show, depict, mention, or discuss violence. Please read with care.

1   Armed Assault

Introduction

Gun violence often affects young people, leaving many with catastrophic injuries that forever alter the course of their lives. Some may never regain the ability to live independently and are forced to reconfigure their entire sense of identity and develop a different plan for the future.

Recovery evolves longitudinally; it often takes years and happens in phases that are unique to every individual. Just as the body takes time to heal, so makes the mind. A person left with a significant disability must redefine every aspect of their life.

The trajectory of one's recovery has everything to do with the quality of support available to them. Family members often step into the role of caregivers. This role is challenging as they must manage extremely painful, shifting emotions, such as grief, rage, or a desire for revenge.[1]

Forgiveness was part of Margaret Long's healing journey. This single word, "forgive," can mean many things. For some, it means to wipe the slate clean, as if the wrong never happened. For others, it means moving past rumination and anger.

Many variables influence how individuals heal from trauma, including the survivor's personality, belief system, and the circumstances of the crime. Did the perpetrator commit the attack in their right mind as purely evil, or were they confused and psychotic? Was remorse expressed after the attack? Did the offender come to accept responsibility, apologize, and attempt to make reparations? The psychological process is complex, and many factors influence it.[2]

We generally think of forgiveness as binary: you either forgive or not. There's no clear demarcation line of demarcation. Margaret's story illustrates a fluctuating process that can be transitory, gradual, temporary, or ephemeral. It ebbs and flows and changes over time. No matter its form, it's always on the survivor's timeline.

Forgiveness may or may not be part of someone's healing journey. We must support each survivor's process, understanding that every path will be unique.

DOI: 10.4324/9781003368137-2

As helpers, we need to encourage survivors to be true to themselves.

On August 11, 1991, two days before her 20th birthday, Margaret Long was shot in the neck by her boyfriend's father, a well-known drug kingpin in Cincinnati's West End neighborhood. The shooting paralyzed her from the chest down. But Margaret turned her suffering into advocacy work, noting that access to guns, especially in tense situations, is dangerous. Her work earned her a Fifth Third Bank Profile in Courage in 2009, and Margaret became Ms. Wheelchair Ohio in 2011.

She joined Moms Demand Action and began working with their volunteers to fight for stricter gun laws in Ohio and nationwide. She traveled with them to Washington, DC to meet with parents who lost children to gun violence and other survivors. She plans to write a book detailing her life story as a survivor and an activist, as well as her relationship with Phelps, her shooter. Margaret believes it will always be a sore subject for her family and his, but the further she distances herself from that fateful night, the more she understands that forgiveness is the right decision.

I Forgave My Shooter and Found Peace

MARGARET LONG

The bullet sliced through my neck and came out of my lower shoulder blade. It took years of physical therapy to regain my mobility, and I still struggle with chronic pain on my left side, which is closest to where the bullet entered. I can't feel my left arm.

Figure 1.1 Scar on Margaret's neck where the bullet went in.
Source: Margaret Long.

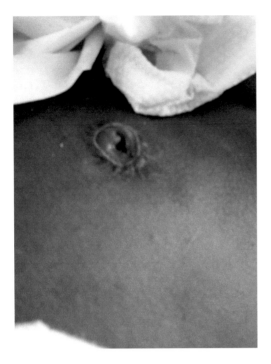

Figure 1.2 Margaret's reconstructed bladder.
Source: Margaret Long.

I have a feeding tube and struggle with recurrent pneumonia because of my paralysis. In addition to my feeding tube, I also urinate through my stomach. I use a catheter that goes into my stomach, emptying my urine into a bag. But I'm alive. And that's what's important.

If I had to live my life all over again, I would've listened to my mother, who warned me not to move to that neighborhood. Shortly before my 20th birthday, I moved to Cincinnati's West End neighborhood, and my life turned for the worse. On August 11, when I was at my sister's house celebrating my birthday, I got drunk. Because of this, my sister did not want me to walk home alone, but I insisted I'd be OK. She tried to stop me a few times from leaving the house, but I ignored her concern.

When I walked home, I ran into my ex-boyfriend, the on-again-off-again one, and we got into an argument. He took out his gun. And I took out my petty little knife. But my ex did the right thing. He placed the gun on the ground because he said he didn't want it to go off accidentally. I also don't think he wanted to hurt me, but we continued to fight. As we fought, someone else picked up the gun. I was not even five feet from my home, and this person fired. They shot me in my neck. My ex put pressure on my neck to slow the bleeding and told my best friend to go get my sister. It didn't take long before the emergency services came.

When I got to the hospital, I didn't know what was happening. I had no idea that I was paralyzed or who had shot me. I later learned that it was my ex-boyfriend's father, Arthur Phelps. He said he was just trying to protect his son. Arthur claimed I pulled a knife on his son and was trying to stab him, but that's not true. Because he claimed self-defense, he was never formally charged.

When I woke up at the hospital, I couldn't speak and could barely move. The doctors thought I wouldn't live, and if I did, I would never be able to walk again or do anything. I don't remember much, except that my family was angry. My brother was furious. He wanted to kill Arthur; he wanted retaliation for what was done to me. But I couldn't talk. I could only blink.

My family asked me, "Do you want us to kill this person that did this to you?"

They told me to blink once for yes and twice for no; that was all I could do. But even with all the pain and the worry about the long recovery ahead, I blinked twice for no. No. No. No. Do not kill this man. They heard me.

The next few years were long and hard, but I did my best. During my recovery, nobody ever came to my family or me and asked if I needed

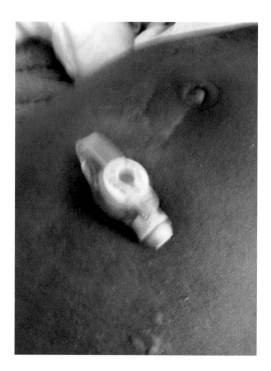

Figure 1.3 Margaret's feeding tube for extra nutrition.
Source: Margaret Long.

Figure 1.4 Margaret at the Ohio pageant.
Source: Margaret Long.

anything. My family and I made it through just by working. I never received any money for victims of crimes. Even when reporters flooded me with questions for their stories, they never asked me if I needed any help. My family helped me. No one else.

Recovery was a beast. But I learned how to use my wheelchair and ask for help. I even went skydiving and regularly participated in pageants.

Then, one day, I turned on the news and saw my shooter, Phelps, on TV talking about preventing gun violence in Cincinnati. That's when I got angry.

I was with my boyfriend at the time, who I'd been with for close to 17 years. We were watching TV when a news segment about gun violence came on. I heard the host of the segment say his name: Phelps.

Damn, I thought. And then newscasters repeated his name. "Hell, no," I said to my boyfriend. "This motherfucker shot me."

I never knew what had happened to him. But that was clear as daylight, and I had my boyfriend tape him using the VCR. "Hurry up, hurry up," I kept telling him. "Put the tape in!"

While the tape was recording, I called my mom. I called my sister. I called everybody.

"Turn the news on. Turn to Channel 12," I screamed through the phone. "Look who that is on TV. Look at the name. That's him," I yelled.

I remember my mother saying, "Oh my God, it *is* him."

My emotions were everywhere. I didn't know if I should cry, laugh, or scream. I wanted to get up and run. I tried to find the man who put me in this chair.

"Where he at?" I screamed. And then I started crying.

I called my sister, who came over immediately to comfort me and provide support. When she got there, she said, "You better stop. Turn the TV off. Turn it off."

I was going skydiving the next day, so she wanted me to stay positive and look forward to tomorrow.

I listened to her. "But keep taping," I cried.

"Calm down," she said. "Don't let him stop you in your tracks. He ain't stopped you once. You ain't going to let him stop you no more. Turn it off or calm down."

After I turned off the TV, my sister asked, "What you going to do?"

"I don't know yet," I shouted. My sister is always the calm one.

"Well, you need to just get calm and get yourself together and get your trip done," she said.

It took me hours to calm down. And my sister and boyfriend stayed with me and helped me through my initial anger and rage.

After taking a breath, I said, "What the hell is he saying? What the fuck is he saying?"

In the segment, Phelps was with the mayor and an unidentified group of people talking about gun violence in Cincinnati. I just kept cussing at the TV. I kept repeating, "This guy is with the mayor, the fucking mayor." This was the guy who put a bullet through my neck, and there he was, standing with Mayor Mark Mallory talking about gun violence prevention.

I didn't know then that Mallory had grown up with my family. My uncles and Mallory were close and spent time together in their youth and adulthood. So, I said to my sister, "We have to call him out."

I called the TV station airing the segment with Phelps and told them what happened to me. I told the girl on the other end of the phone, "This man you have on TV with the mayor now is the man that shot me."

I asked her, "Where's this man at? What group was he with on the TV?"

"The Urban League," she told me. And she gave me their contact number. This was a group I always wanted to get involved with. I'd always see them on TV chanting, "Stop the violence, stop the killing, stop the violence." And I wanted to get into one of these groups.

When I called the Urban League and told a rep what happened to me and that my shooter had been on TV with the mayor and their group, they said, "Don't say nothing else. I want you to talk to the boss."

I told the boss everything that happened to me. I told him what I told his rep.

"We had our one-year anniversary of the ceasefire," he said. "Would you like to come and speak?"

I was like, "Well, yeah. I want him to see what he did to me."

"OK, I'm going to set it up," he said.

On the day of the Community Initiative to Reduce Violence event, organized by the Urban League, news crews had gotten wind that I was meeting my shooter for the first time since he shot me. Honestly, I didn't know what to say to them. *How should I act?* I thought. *How should I respond to their questions?* I was overwhelmed with emotion.

When I got off the bus, my sister and her boyfriend, Wayne, were waiting for me. Wayne was crazy. He wanted to kill Phelps.

"Look, Wayne, don't touch this man," I pleaded. "I'm not even thinking about hurting this man for real."

Phelps walked up to me and kissed me when we got into this event.

Oh, hell no, I said to myself. I don't know why, but I faked it for the cameras. I returned his kiss with a small peck on his cheek. He laid into me hard, hugging me tightly, and I had my arm on his. And I'm just playing to the camera thinking, *What the fuck am I doing? Is this real? Just get it over with*.

The reporters were excited. They are always hungry for this kind of shit. They kept saying, "This never happens!" and "I can't believe you are facing the man who shot you."

And then it poured out of me. I couldn't hide my anger. "I wanted him to see what he did," I told the gaggle of reporters. "He thought I was dead," I said. "I'm right here."

Phelps looked at me and cried. I'm just watching him, looking at him, still thinking, *Is this real?* It was. Very.

He just kept talking nervously. It was as if he was saying sorry, but he wasn't saying sorry.

"Like, I just don't know what to say. I don't know how. I will be there for you," he whispered.

I watched him as he faked an apology. I stayed silent and thought *Bullshit. Whatever you say.*

But what was supposed to be a one-time meeting turned into a request from the League to make more appearances with Phelps, my shooter. The League reasoned that it was positive because we never heard somebody forgiving their shooter, speaking with them, walking together, and trying to help the neighborhood.

I'm doing this for the kids, I thought. And so I forgave him, believing his day would come.

We went ahead and worked together. We went to detention centers, the courthouse, and schools. We went to a lot of high schools. And he'll tell his part, and then I'll tell mine. We even had a gospel rapper performing at the event. But as we spoke together, his story constantly changed. First, he said I was in the way of getting to his dope because he was an extensive dealer then, and then he said it was in self-defense of his son, claiming I was going to stab him. I still say he needs to make up his mind about what he did that fucking night and tell the truth. He shot me because he wanted some damn drugs. That's the truth.

He was a known kingpin in Cincinnati. He brought the drugs to the city. He brought the guns to the city. He got the women on drugs. He had kids out there selling drugs, women, and guns. Everybody used to call him Pops. He was known. Everybody knew this man. He had a record.

That's how he got into the Urban League because he was the exact person they were looking for as a role model. Phelps was in Lucasville Prison when they had a riot. And due to him not getting involved in the riot and not trying to escape, he got time off for good behavior. That's how he got out of prison. He didn't get any time for shooting me because he played nice in prison.

The courts never told me why he didn't get any time. But something told me to get on my computer and investigate. The only thing I could find via public record on my shooting was that he was only charged with assault, not attempted murder. I tried calling the police, but they bounced me around.

Six months later, I checked back on the computer: he got all his criminal activity expunged. My friends and family would ask me if I wanted to reopen the case, but I declined. Phelps looked sick. I knew he wasn't doing well. He seemed haggard and lost. My heart told me to let it go. Let him go.

People still want to kill him. My current boyfriend wants to kill him. My brother still wants to kill him. And then the tears just start falling down my face because I feel like my family was wronged and they are hurting. No one helped us. The city failed us. And that's when a local organization found me. They encouraged me to go to City Hall one day and I was just in my feelings, and I was just going *there*.

"You know what? Y'all failed my family," I said. I looked at every mayor, every city councilor in their faces. I stared at them.

I said it again, "Y'all failed my family. Y'all failed my family and me because y'all didn't lock up the man who shot me. He didn't get a day in jail, but I've been suffering every day in this wheelchair. Surgery after surgery. Hospital stays. My family's got to stay in the hospital all night. They've got to hold the bucket for me to throw up. They've got to sit there and hold my hand while I cry. When I fall, they pick me up."

They were quiet as usual.

The last I heard of Phelps is that he's sick. He has Alzheimer's or dementia. I hate to say it, but it's karma. But I'm still close with his son. My sister knows that we are friends, and we will stay friends because he always said he would be my friend forever.

"I'm not going to leave you," he said after I was shot.

I know it's bad what happened, but we don't discuss it. He didn't do it; he didn't shoot me. He took care of me and feels really bad about what happened.

It's hard staying positive about my situation. I feel like nothing has changed in the 30 years since I was shot. But I'm at peace.

I'm still here.

I'm still going.

That's something.

Notes

1 Stéphane Guay, Valérie Billette and André Marchand. "Exploring the Links between Posttraumatic Stress Disorder and Social Support: Processes and Potential Research Avenues." *Journal of Traumatic Stress*, 19(3): 327–38, 2006. www.acade mia.edu/13816414/Exploring_the_links_between_posttraumatic_stress_dis-order_and_social_support_Processes_and_potential_research_avenues.
2 Berthold P. R. Gersons and Miranda Olff. "Coping with the Aftermath of Trauma." *BMJ*, 330(7499): 1038–9, 2005. www.bmj.com/content/330/7499/1038.

2 Armed Intruder

Introduction

As victims of armed intruders, Caia DelaVergne and Darien Richardson fought hard to survive. They had very different outcomes.

Caia presents a vivid example of the body's innate stress response, *fight-flight-freeze*. This response occurs without conscious awareness in times of danger. Humans have evolved to survive catastrophes, and the stress response helps us to do so.[1] Caia's brain went to a *freeze* response, and she moved to *flee*. She was active and persistent, despite her massive injury.

Though this stress response is adaptive during moments of danger, our bodies dislike living in this state of physical and emotional dysregulation for extended periods. While physical injuries need expedient treatment, emotional support is also essential in helping return the body and mind to a state of calm regulation. Victims need to be comforted, soothed, listened to, and reassured; we can enhance the process as we interact with them by remaining calm and ensuring they are not left alone. Conversational distraction often works well in helping the parasympathetic nervous system do its job. Just having a compassionate human presence is powerful. Our tone of voice matters as much as the words we say, as their nervous system will respond to our nervous system.[2]

Caia spent 12 hours with catastrophic injuries in an emergency room with no way to contact her family or friends. She was isolated. This isolation kept her in a state of autonomic hyperarousal. It would have been immensely beneficial for her to have a support person during this time.

Enhancing emotional support for hospitalized victims of violence is critical to healing. Without help, the violence survivor may continue in a state of heightened autonomic arousal, which can intensify multiple physical and psychological symptoms.[3]

Healing is our natural inclination once we are no longer in danger. Caia said, "I finally felt like I could breathe" once the perpetrator had been tried and convicted. When she felt safe, her body and mind returned to a place of balanced regulation.

DOI: 10.4324/9781003368137-3

Judi Richardson, Darien's mother, describes her daughter's classic symptoms of PTSD—flashbacks, nightmares, and multiple related physical symptoms. After a catastrophic injury, the mind and body must heal simultaneously, and we must pay attention to both.

Judi's story illustrates the healing power of family support and emotional attunement. Nurturing relationships facilitate the healing process. In the Richardson family, all members came together to help Darien recover. Not all families have the resources to do this. The Richardsons are a highly connected family, and each one felt Darien's pain. There is more than one victim whenever a person is wounded; everyone who loves them suffers.

The Richardson family story also shows how loved ones long for closure when a perpetrator is never arrested and the reasons for the attack are never known. Without this closure, echoes of the trauma follow them throughout their daily lives as they struggle to contain anxiety and make sense of what happened.

Caia DelaVergne screamed before she was shot in the face. She was 19 and had just moved back to her hometown of Anchorage, Alaska, to

Figure 2.1 Caia's eye wound and scar.
Source: Caia DelaVergne.

attend college. On October 23, 2015, Caia and her male friend were just two teenagers enjoying some gossip and a movie when an uninvited acquaintance with a .45 caliber handgun forcibly entered her friend's house. The bullet tore through her left eye and skull and came out the back of her neck. Her friend was also shot.

"After he shot me, I pretended to be dead," says Caia. "I held still until he left. I watched him disappear from the room like a ghost back into blackness," she adds.

Every second on the floor felt like an eternity for Caia as she waited for her shooter to leave. Confident he was gone, she reached for her cell phone buried deep inside her pocket. With all her strength, she dialed 911.

I Was Shot By a Man I Thought Was My Friend

CAIA DELAVERGNE

"What's your emergency?" said the operator.

The wound to my face prevented me from saying, "Help."

Their repeated questions, "Hello, anyone there? What's your emergency?" only frustrated me more.

I tried to ask for help again. Then there was silence and a dial tone. It was then I realized that no one was coming.

Before getting shot, I was just watching a movie with my friend. Then there was a fierce and fast banging at the front door. Then silence. And again, more banging, but now at the back door, the doorknob shook this time. He tried to get in once, but this time he was successful.

The staircase squeaked as an unidentified person entered. Then he was, a guy I'd met only three weeks ago at a party, who I thought was a new friend. He pointed his .45 caliber black handgun at me and didn't say a word.

After my call to 911 failed, I picked myself up off the floor. I grabbed a towel from the laundry basket, wrapped it around my head, opened the window, and climbed out. Pain shot through my neck as I squeezed out of the window. I later learned this pain was a result of the exit wound.

I slowly lowered myself out of the second-story window and jumped, landing butt-first in a bush. As I lay there in branches and leaves, I saw the man who shot me run out of the house to his truck. My friend was still inside; I was worried he'd already died. But for me to get help, I had to stay alive. I hid in the bushes until the shooter was gone and then ran into the freezing October night, frantically flagging down every passing car for help. But no car stopped, and I was starting to lose hope that I'd be helped or that my friend would get the help he needed.

So, I took a more aggressive approach and walked into the middle of the road. They'd either stop or run me over; I took my chances. Finally, someone stopped. I remember telling Lou, the man who stopped his car, "I'm shot."

Almost immediately after arriving in the ER, the police questioned me. One officer confiscated my phone for evidence. Now phoneless, I couldn't even contact my family, who were abroad in Japan for work. After a long 12 hours, my godmother was finally notified, and she came to meet me at the hospital. They said my neck was broken. I still had blood all over my face and body and sticks in my hair from the bush I landed in. My godmother and the nurses told me not to look in the mirror, but I looked anyway. Covered in dried blood and dirt, my face was bruised and swollen; I didn't recognize myself. When I left the hospital three days later, my family had covered all the mirrors in my house. Looking at my face scared me.

After a 15-hour manhunt and a high-speed chase, the shooter was finally apprehended by police.

His trial for my and my friend's attempted murder was postponed for almost three years because the shooter filed unnecessary motions to control us from jail. My life was on hold. But in October 2018, the man who shot my friend and me was finally sentenced to 141 years with 60 years suspended, making his total time to be served 81 years.

At trial, I learned that after he shot my friend and me, he went to his parents' house, where they let him shower and wash away evidence of the attempted double murder he had just committed. He admitted to his parents what he'd done, and they encouraged him to flee instead of calling the police. During this time at his parents' house, he posted on Facebook, writing that my friend got what he deserved. Word for word, this is what he wrote, "That's what happens to people that fuck around with the girl I'm with behind my back. They catch Bullets. Im a wanted fugitive and felon now. Oh well! If they want me come an get me unload this clip till its empty."

In addition to the Facebook post, he texted my friends and me saying he was happy we were both alive because now he could "come back and finish the job."

After the shooting, I received a prosthetic eye, which most people didn't notice was fake. They mostly assumed I had a lazy eye. But those assumptions felt like judgments. When I moved back to the small military base in Japan with my mom, it seemed everyone knew what had happened. There were times I walked around the base and heard comments like, "That's the girl who was shot!" I felt ostracized. This was less than a year post-shooting, and I was still healing physically and emotionally. Even now, I'm still healing, but I'm an active advocate for gun reform.

After the trial and sentencing, I felt like I could breathe again. I imagine it felt the same for my friend. But the trial was traumatizing. The defense blamed my friend and me for the shooter's actions. They weaved lies about an unstable person who felt "lost and lonely," as if he were the victim. But no one was convinced: not the jury, and I don't even think his lawyer was convinced. I know that if I had not escaped to find help, my friend and I would be dead. Somehow we made it. I wish that were true for others who did not survive their wounds.

> On January 8, 2010, at 1:30 AM, armed intruders broke into Darien Richardson's home in Portland, Maine, guns blazing, recalls her mother, Judi Richardson. They fired shots into Darien's bedroom, shattering her thumb while she tried to shield herself from the bullets.
>
> As she tried to roll off the bed to hide, another bullet struck her right leg through her knee, traveled the length of her thigh, and lodged in her hip. Another bullet grazed her boyfriend's shoulder as he hid beside the bed.
>
> Darien spent three days in the ICU, 18 days in critical care, and spent the weeks that followed working through the emotional and physical pain resulting from severe trauma. "Those weeks were harrowing for Darien and our family," Judi says. "She had pins in her thumb and external steel fixation that had to be soaked and painfully cleaned daily," she adds.
>
> Tragically, on February 28, 2010, 51 days after Darien was shot, she died from complications from her gunshot wounds. She was only 25. Her murder remains unsolved.

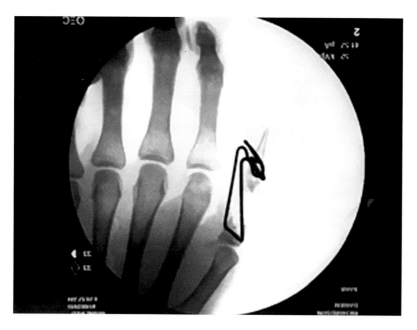

Figure 2.2 The bullet shattered Darien Richardson's thumb.
Source: Judi Richardson.

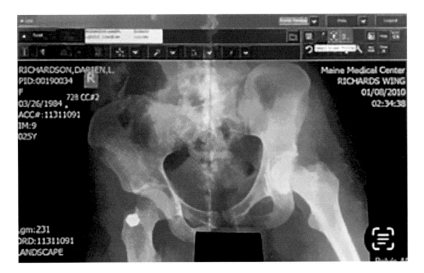

Figure 2.3 The bullet in Darien Richardson's right hip.
Source: Judi Richardson.

Where the Bullet Enters

JUDI RICHARDSON

My daughter, Darien, had a large open wound where the bullet entered on January 8, 2010, which needed to be packed and changed every four hours. The pin care and wound care were excruciating. Doctors put her on complete bed rest. In addition to her injuries' physical pain, she suffered from severe PTSD and experienced vivid, disturbing dreams of a door opening and seeing herself covered in blood. She was stressed out and had no appetite or energy. She felt helpless and frustrated but put on a brave face and stayed positive. I took a leave from work and stayed with her every day and night at the hospital.

We huddled as a family. Her sister, Sarena, and her dad, Wayne, were there in the evenings after work and every day off. Darien could not do all the little self-care because her left hand was useless. Her sister washed her and styled her hair so lovingly. We poured all our love into her to let her know she wasn't going through this alone. We wanted her to feel safe and know that we supported her, loved her, and were in this together. I believed all we had to do was *love* her, and she'd be whole again. But it wasn't that easy.

Darien had physical therapy to learn to walk again. After some weeks, they discharged her from the hospital when she could finally walk. We were very concerned about her discharge. I thought it was too soon. The physical therapist said we could continue at home and the nurse taught me how to change the dressing and pack the wound in her thigh as well as clean the pins in her thumb and hand. They also helped me set up visits to the surgery trauma care outpatient center for additional help. Darien understood she had a long way to go to recover and more surgeries in her future, but she was willing to work to heal.

The second surgery date for her hand was scheduled, and we all hoped that a bone graft from her wrist or hip would replace the middle bone in her thumb. But we knew her knuckle in that thumb was utterly ruptured, so she would never regain the full ability to bend or grasp with it.

Her physical wounds, though, were just one part of her trauma. She was addressing her PTSD with therapy sessions and medication. She was doing everything right. However, 51 days after the shooting, she tragically died from delayed complications related to her gunshot wounds. She died on February 28, 2010. She was only 25.

Darien's death devastated our family and me. Not a day goes by that we don't feel her absence in the world and the space where she should be. The heartbreak and loss continue as time passes because Darien's life is cut too short. Darien couldn't see her beautiful sister get married; she should've been there with us when her sister took her vows. She should be here now.

The following is what I want to tell the shooters.

Darien had her entire life ahead of her and so much more to contribute to the world. Darien was beautiful (inside and out), vibrant with a zest for life. Darien was loving, kind, helpful, and generous. Darien's big, bright, infectious smile drew everyone to her. Darien sought out and found only the good in everyone she met, always showing love and compassion to all around her. Darien was a social butterfly who loved music and loved to dance. Darien was also intelligent, accomplished, hardworking, independent, and a valued member of our society. Darien was loved and missed by all who knew her.

She was robbed of her life, independence, use of her left hand, and ability to feel safe, sleep peacefully, and ability to do dancing.

Words cannot describe the physical, and emotional pain, grief, and trauma that Darien endured that night and all those weeks or the pain we have lived with since her death. You didn't just shoot and kill our daughter/sister Darien; you murdered our entire family. Our joy, our future, and our past all painfully changed. We will never be the same. We miss her so much that there are no words to express it adequately. There is no way to effectively convey how we have been affected.

At 25, Darien was a successful young woman with many friends, her apartment, and a successful career. Darien's world turned upside down in just a few minutes. She couldn't work, she couldn't return to her apartment, and she had to move back home with her father and me. She looked at a long recovery and lots of financial losses and expenses. Watching Darien suffer was horrific. I took weeks off from work and seemed to live without sleep to keep her well. Yet it wasn't enough, and she died.

After her death, I was too distraught to function; I was physically and emotionally gone and done. I couldn't get out of bed. I didn't want to leave the house. I didn't want to see anyone. The pain was visceral. Sarena's only sibling has been taken from her and will not be around to grow old with and experience all the joys that sisters share. Our family is not the same without her. We're not the same people as we were before. The pain is just below the surface, even in fun times (and there are some).

In the years since her death, we continue to be re-victimized by the police investigation, now a cold case, an unsolved homicide. We continue to feel the pain of not knowing who shot her. How do we seek justice? *Who are you?* Knowing you are walking the streets after committing this crime is unbearable. You could be behind us in line at the grocery store, the pharmacy, or at our door.

We have always been private people, working and raising our families. Now our privacy is gone. Victims are constantly re-victimized in our society. Simple, everyday pleasures in life, like going for a walk, eating a favorite food, or asking someone how they are, can be heartbreaking endeavors. The trauma and experience are constantly on my mind. People, even friends, and family, don't fully understand our pain. The pain you brought us.

We were victimized twice by not knowing who killed our daughter and never having an opportunity to find justice for her. But it seems that not even the state of Maine is concerned about you being free and roaming the streets.

Please, do not do this to another family.

I want you to know that our daughter, our beautiful Darien, didn't die immediately. She suffered greatly before passing.

After her death, our family formed a foundation in her honor to help those affected by and wounded by gun violence. We have become activists for better gun safety laws nationally and in our state. We have advocated for a cold case unit in our state and victims' rights laws. Why do we have a criminal justice system but not a victims' justice system in this country?

I want you to know that I ask the same daily questions: What would Darien have accomplished in the last 13 years? What would Darien look like now? Would she be married, have a house, or have kids? How many fun birthdays and holidays would our family have continued to enjoy as we did when we were whole? What fun we would have had with her on her sister's wedding trip to Mexico, and how excited she would have been supporting her sister during her pregnancy and becoming an aunt for the first time.

I also ask what it would feel like to have not lived with this pain all these years. What would it be like to have been happy all these years? We work to protect our children from bikes, cars, drowning, alcohol, drugs, strangers, and other dangers, but we do nothing to protect them from gun violence.

I admit, I didn't pay full attention until it affected Darien and our family, until you took her from us. Gun homicides, suicides, unintentional shootings of children, unsecured-gun "accidents," police shootings, and domestic violence shootings leave behind the same pain as the mass shootings that are more likely to gather the public attention and make the news. Every shooting is the most devastating to the victim and their family, and our response to this pain and trauma should reflect that truth.

I hope one day you'll come forward and bring some type of closure to the horror me and my family go through as well as justice for Darien. I hope you'll realize that where a bullet enters is not always where it stays. That bullet goes through everyone who loves that person. That bullet makes a giant hole in the hearts and minds of those left living.

Notes

1 John J. Donahue. "Fight-Flight-Freeze System." In V. Zeigler-Hill and T. K. Shackelford (eds.), *Encyclopedia of Personality and Individual Differences*. Cham: Springer, 2020, 1590–5. https://doi.org/10.1007/978-3-319-24612-3_751.
2 Bonnie Badenoch. *Being a Brain-Wise Therapist: A Practical Guide to Interpersonal Neurobiology*. New York: W. W. Norton, 2008.
3 Jonathan I. Bisson, Sarah Cosgrove, Catrin Lewis and Neil P. Roberts. "Post-Traumatic Stress Disorder." *BMJ*, 351, 2015. https://doi.org/10.1136/bmj.h6161.

3 Armed Robbery

Introduction

Shot in an armed robbery, Kevin Neary was left wondering if his life was worth living. Multiple operations later—more than he can count—he has concluded that it is. Now, Kevin sees that his physical limitations do not define him. He also understands that he would not be where he is now without the love and support of his family.

The damage Kevin sustained physically has left him in need of 24-hour care in the ten years since his shooting. Mainly, his family members provided his care. Kevin's story illustrates how the power of an attuned, loving, and dedicated family and excellent rehab care has kept Kevin psychologically well.

The discipline of interpersonal neurobiology offers helpful and hopeful information for those who would support trauma survivors. This interdisciplinary field focuses on how our brain, body, and mind develop into a neurobiological system and how this system continually evolves in the context of our relationships with others.[1]

Humans nearby naturally synchronize heart rates, breathing, and movement as their neurobiological systems align. Without realizing it, our brains grow and change as we exchange energy and information with those nearby. When we keep our nervous systems in a state of calm regulation, others naturally begin to experience increased regulation in *their* nervous systems simply from being in *our* presence.[2]

Just as trauma can shape our brains, new experiences and relationships also reshape them. Positive relationships centered on empathy are the foundation of healing.

A decade later, Kevin is still occasionally haunted by "what ifs." Of course, he sometimes wonders what his life would have looked like if he'd not encountered the man with the gun.

Despite the resulting physical disabilities and episodic times of despair, Kevin is still Kevin. As he puts it, "My diagnosis does not define me." Kevin finds tremendous meaning in the quality of his relationships with his loved ones and in offering hope to others.

DOI: 10.4324/9781003368137-4

The night of Monday, November 14, 2011, Kevin had gone to the Penn State University basketball game, then met up with a friend in his neighborhood (Northern Liberties). After walking his friend home and spending time hanging out, Kevin was followed for several blocks by Christopher Easton, then age 20. When Kevin was just steps away from the entrance to his building, Easton shot Kevin in an attempted robbery. Kevin was conscious when the police arrived but lost consciousness on the way to the hospital. The Philadelphia Police were able to identify a suspect and were able to locate him reasonably quickly with the help of the news media and the many people who helped find him. Contributions may be made to Kevin Neary Trust, Box 1824, Upper Chichester, PA 19061, or at http://kevinneary.com/kevin-neary-trust.

I Was Going to Live, Right?

KEVIN NEARY

Soon after I arrived at the hospital, it became clear to the doctors that there was significant damage to my spinal column. The bullet ripped through my spinal cord at the C5 level, leaving me paralyzed below the neck. Although the injury was initially thought to be at the C5 level, the percussive effects of the bullet injured my spinal cord up to the C2 level, which means I need assistance from a ventilator or a pacer device to breathe. This shooting was a little over ten and a half years ago.

I became a victim of a gunshot wound during an attempted robbery on my way home from an evening with friends. Just around the corner from my apartment, I was pushed from behind. When I turned around, there was a gun pointed at me. I exchanged words with the assailant, but it was evident to me that I was in danger. Shortly after that, he pulled the trigger.

Before the accident, I had begun working as a recruiter. In 2010, I started working independently to develop my own successful business. In addition to recruiting, I waited tables during the off hours to help support my day-to-day needs. I could see reasons to be excited about the future and make my goal of assisting others in making their current career path a reality.

After the gunshot, I remember lying on the ground, unable to feel my arms or legs. I tried to call for help, but my voice seemed weaker with each attempt. A few minutes later, I opened my eyes and saw a police officer (or maybe an EMT) kneeling next to me. I remember pleading with him not to let me die. The next thing I knew, I was in the back of an ambulance on the way to the emergency department.

I stayed at three hospitals: Hahnemann University Hospital, Jefferson University Hospital, and Magee Rehabilitation Hospital. The first was Hahnemann, a trauma center, where they preserved my life. I was transferred to Jefferson because of its reputation as a spinal cord injury center. After I was stabilized in the ICU, I was transferred to Magee, where I began learning how to transition from the hospital to home care.

Life was rough for some time. I remember periods of intense sedation from all the medications administered. There were also many moments when I experienced significant amounts of pain. One of the most frustrating effects of my injury was initially losing the ability to speak. I recall being in the hospital when the police questioned me, and I could not respond verbally. I had to look at mugshots of suspects, remember what my shooter looked like, and use head movements or some other cue instead of relying upon my voice. At other times, I had to use an alphabet board to spell out my answers or mouth words so people could read my lips.

I think it was when I was in Jefferson that I realized that the likelihood I would ever walk again was very slim. It made me question my life. I never wanted to live like this, nor did I want to live in a paralyzed condition. How could this happen? I was terrified of what my life would be like now that I could not walk or do the things that I would normally do, like get out of bed, my two feet feeling the cold floor. I felt like I was living someone else's life. Sometimes I wondered if I would have been better off if I had passed away.

I required several operations, more than I can count, including procedures to stabilize my neck, install a pacemaker, and keep my airway open, to name a few. As a result, I had a lot to learn. The staff at Magee Rehabilitation Hospital pushed me forward and kept me going. I learned everything I needed to know to direct my care and survive in a home setting. I am incredibly grateful for the staff there and the friendships I developed with them. During the last few days at Magee, my family brought t-shirts for all the nurses and the hospital staff who helped me. On the shirts was a message: Friends of Kevin Neary. These were the shirts that we used for one of our first fundraisers.

From there, I returned home, where my father and family, with the assistance of home health nursing, assumed the responsibility of caring for me around the clock. To avoid pressure sores and keep my muscles from contracting, I needed to be repositioned often and assisted with a basic range of motion. When in bed, I reposition every two hours, and when in the wheelchair, every 30 minutes. At the same time, they were also helping me take my medications. There were many medications, ranging from muscle relaxants to minimize the number of muscle spasms, blood thinners to prevent blood clots, a blood-pressure drug to combat low-pressure levels, sleep medicine, and many others.

Over ten years later, I still rely upon assistive technology to breathe. During the day, I use a phrenic nerve pacer, an external device that stimulates my diaphragm, enabling me to breathe independently. At night, I use a ventilator to assist my breathing passively. I require assistance to eat, bathe, and perform many of the simple tasks I would commonly do on a day-to-day basis. Fortunately, I have movement from the shoulders and above, which enables me to use a power wheelchair with my head.

There are many days I wonder what it would have been like if I had never encountered Christopher Easton if I had walked down a different path or headed home earlier. However, the reality remains that it happened, and my condition results from those events. At the time, the wounds from the gunshot, the wounds from the various surgical procedures, and the emotional wounds that accompanied them made me feel as if I had lost everything. It was hard to accept that I would not have the ability to be as active as I was.

Most of my medical bills are paid through Medicare and, in some circumstances, waiver programs. The rest are paid for by money from various fundraisers and the generosity of many friends and family. We established a special needs trust that is used for the additional expenses of medications and other basic needs that are not covered through insurance. I have had the good fortune of having my story covered by various news outlets that called attention to my case and brought awareness to my situation. I also benefited from the charity of so many people who contributed their time and various skills to build an addition to the house that includes a bedroom, living room, outside deck, and spacious shower room that can accommodate a shower trolley that I lie on for bathing in the mornings.

It might seem complicated for some people to understand, but I now know this is not the worst of fates. While I struggled with whether or not life is worth living, I realized that I have a great support system. My brothers, Joe and Chris, have been a light for my father and me. As my primary caregiver, he retired to assume responsibility for overseeing my care so I could stay at home and avoid living in a nursing home. My family's commitment made me realize that I am fortunate to have a better situation than many.

Looking back, I see how far I have come. Often, I remind myself that my diagnosis does not define me. I know what will define me is what I do in the future. I know I am where I am today because of the love and support of my friends and family and my desire to see certain things happen in my lifetime. I have had the opportunity to see my family grow, first with my brothers' spouses and then with the addition of three nephews.

Fundraising is just one of the many things that help me. My amazing group of friends and family help me the most, keeping my spirits high and encouraging me to do as much as possible to get out into the community. Unfortunately, my story is similar to many. Hopefully, I can show others who have experienced injuries like mine that life is beyond our condition. Life will never be the same; however, we can find comfort through the friends and family who care so much for us.

Notes

1 Daniel J. Siegel. *The Developing Mind: How Relationships and the Brain Interact to Shape Who We Are*, 3rd edition. New York: Guilford Publications, 2020.
2 Bonnie Badenoch. *Being a Brain-Wise Therapist: A Practical Guide to Interpersonal Neurobiology*. New York: W. W. Norton, 2008.

4   Domestic Violence

Introduction

There are similarities among most victims of intimate partner violence. They experience repeated coercion, control, threats, and bullying patterns that often alternate with increasingly brief times when their partners make them feel loved and supported. The abusers usually have two distinct personalities: kind and loving, rageful and sadistic.[1]

Living with a partner like this causes confusion, PTSD, dissociation, and a loss of a sense of agency and control over one's life. Victims of verbal abuse, threats, and physical violence may quickly feel a sense of powerlessness as they accept blame for the abuse and try to modify their behavior to keep the abuser from getting angry.[2]

Whether violent episodes are frequent or rare, the confusion experienced by those in such relationships is overwhelming. The psychological manipulation is constant and ongoing, and the victim's life increasingly becomes prison-like. For example, Kate Ranta experienced feelings of being trapped with an abuser.

When people ask, "Why doesn't the abuse victim just leave?" it's clear that they don't understand that leaving can have deadly consequences. The most dangerous time in an abusive relationship is when the victim attempts to escape. Victims understand that abusers are likely to follow through on their threats. They realize that they or their children are in danger if they try to leave.[3]

Abusers often threaten to take custody of their children. They ensure the victim loses access to financial resources. If a victim does not have family resources, they may fear homelessness. The abuser has often cut them off from their family and friends, so their support system is minimal, and they may have no financial resources.

Leaving is not only dangerous for the victim—20% of the time, family members of the victim are killed when a victim tries to leave the relationship.[4]

The person living in this kind of relationship feels shame on many levels. They blame themselves for what happened and for being in the relationship. Shame results in isolation as they keep what's happening a secret.

DOI: 10.4324/9781003368137-5

Kate's story illustrates the capacity of a dangerously pathological predator driven by control and rage. Many people like this appear normal to people outside of their intimate relationships. After a spousal murder, it's common for others to say, "but he [the perpetrator] seemed like such a nice guy." But even as Kate Ranta's abuser brutalized her entire family, the family continued to work together to recover.

Clai Lasher-Sommers lived with pervasive abuse as a child in her family of origin, ultimately being shot by her stepfather as an adolescent. When children grow up with chronic abuse, it impacts their development on multiple levels. They learn to expect abuse, that those who claim to love them will hurt them, and that hypervigilance is required to survive. The fight-flight response becomes their baseline; everything in life that comes easily to others is more difficult for them.[5] Building a successful life as an adult takes tremendous work for the individual with a history of chronic childhood abuse.

Despite the trauma history, Clai found a path to healing. She has used her lived experience to help others and bring social change. She has dedicated years of her life to advocacy and social justice work focused on helping victims of many kinds of violence. She has also been an activist in advancing gun safety legislation. Clai has used her voice, found agency, and continues her healing journey.

> In 2012—after leaving an emotionally, financially, and sexually abusive marriage—Kate Ranta's ex-husband stalked her to her apartment in Parkland, FL, where he shot her and her father twice. He shot them in front of Kate's then-four-year-old son, William. One bullet destroyed her right hand, and another went through her left breast, just missing her heart. Her father, Rob Ranta, was shot in his left arm, which is still disabled, and on his left side, just missing his heart and lung. Although not physically hurt, Kate's son witnessed the entire event from start to finish. Kate's mother, Susan Ranta, continues to be a lifeline for the family, holding them close and together. These are their stories. "The bullets tore through my home, cut through my sacred, safe space. It was as if I was watching a movie," writes Kate Ranta. "The scene featuring me is very dramatic, a mixture of both fast and slow motion."

Ranta Strong: A Family Essay in Three POVs

KATE RANTA, ROBERT RANTA AND SUSAN RANTA

This Isn't Happening

KATE RANTA

The bullets tore through my home while my four-year-old son watched *Spiderman*.

"Shit, *he* found me!"

My head spun, and my hands shook.

I was more than a year into a contentious divorce with my husband, who had become physically and emotionally abusive throughout our three-year marriage. I wanted to move on, but he and his scumbag divorce lawyer had other plans. He wanted the house, which I gave him. But that wasn't enough.

He found me within two weeks of moving into my own apartment in a secret location with my son. In the month leading up to November 2, 2012, my ex-husband's threatening behavior escalated. He texted and emailed me nonstop.

"I'm going to take William away from you," he texted late one night. "And when I do, I'll win in court." I read his text over and over again, terrified he might win. How could he be so smug? So heartless? It wasn't that he cared about William; he wanted to hurt me.

After I moved, there were several instances of damage to my car. He let the air out of my tires, ripped the air conditioner unit, and dented the doors. But I couldn't prove *he* did those things, which made it hard for the police to do anything. But I knew. It was him messing with me.

But the night he shot me, my tire pressure was low before leaving to meet with some friends for dinner. My heart pounded. When I stepped out of the car, I found a long gash in the front passenger tire. *SHIT.*

I phoned my dad. "I'll be right over," he said with urgency. "Call the police and report it."

I called, even though I knew they'd do nothing. I had no restraining order in place. I was turned down for three permanent orders after my temporary one expired.

When my dad arrived, he took William inside the house while I spoke with the young female officer. I explained my estranged husband's violent domestic history, including the time he tried to kidnap our son, the Child Protective Services charges against him for giving William unprescribed medications, and his many violations of established restraining orders.

"He has vandalized my car before," I told the officer. "There was no way anybody else would have sliced my tire."

I paused.

Almost in tears, I said, "He's letting me know he found me."

But rather than comforting me or coming up with a solution, she asked, "Do you have a restraining order?"

I sighed. "No. I've been turned down multiple times."

"Ma'am, there is nothing I can do," she said.

It was the same old chatter I'd been dealing with for the past year and a half.

She never asked to see a photo of him. She never asked what kind of car he drove. And she never offered to patrol my complex to know if he was on it.

Instead, she gave me a record number and encouraged me to visit the courthouse the next day and apply for a restraining order.

Before she left, I made sure she knew it was serious, saying, "He is going to have to kill me before you people do anything about him."

No response.

I walked back into my apartment, where my dad sat with William. I was frustrated and scared. We rolled our eyes in unison when I told my dad about the conversation with the officer. My dad and mom had often been to this rodeo with our local police.

Before returning home, my dad suggested I call for roadside assistance. "After it's fixed, meet your mom and me at home," he said.

I watched him walk into the night, but he turned back. My father's pale face shone back at me. He said, "Kate, call 911. Tom is here."

I looked out the door and saw my ex's BMW backed up against my car. When his dome light came on, I knew it was him.

"Go inside, Kate," he yelled.

"Dad, come inside with me," I screamed back.

I toggled between watching my father with Tom and yelling at the 911 operator, "Someone please, please, please come. My, my ex-husband is here."

But how quickly things turned. As my voice cracked with desperation into the phone, my father rushed towards the door, and Tom followed. I hung up with the operator to help my dad close the door while my ex tried to push his way inside. But he didn't need to push; he had a gun and shot through the door, hitting my dad and me.

My estranged husband's child, my four-year-old son, stood just a few feet behind me. I howled like a wolf. And then he fired the gun a second time. My right hand exploded.

"Please, Tom!" I screamed and begged. "Please, stop!"

He leaned down close to my cheek. "Why did you take my stuff?" he said calmly. I could feel his breath. "Was it worth it, you fucking bitch?"

"I'm sorry, I'm sorry! Tom, I'm sorry!" I screamed back. "I'll give it back! I'll return it!" The *stuff* he was referring to was furniture I'd taken from our marital home when I moved out, which I'd bought myself. But that didn't matter to him. He considered everything his, even people.

On the ground, I couldn't move my right arm. My clothes stuck to me like fly paper, and the iron smell of my blood filled my nose. As I crawled around the kitchenette table, bleeding out, my hand dangled like a loose light on a string. I sat shaking, waiting for the kill shot.

I heard my dad grunting. *He killed my father*, I thought. But I didn't know for sure.

In shock, my son stood on the opposite side of the table from me. Tom knelt next to William and taunted me with the laser on his big black gun.

"Don't do it, Daddy! Don't shoot Mommy!" William squealed.

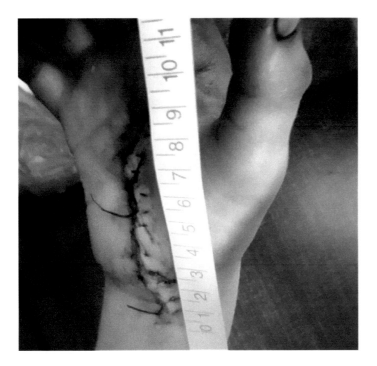

Figure 4.1 Kate's bullet wound post-surgery.
Source: Kate Ranta.

Tom walked to the front door and peeked outside. He knew law enforcement had arrived. Sirens blared through the windows, and police lights filled the small living room.

"Kate, there's a runner on the table. Grab it and wrap the wound."

I did as Tom said. I felt myself fade.

"Kate, go. Just go," he said, coaching me to my death. But I wouldn't. I didn't want to die. Instead, I forced myself to crawl to the door and past Tom, who'd already surrendered to the police. I later found out that officers found extra ammunition and a hunting knife on him along with the 9mm Beretta he used to shoot us.

"Ma'am, can you get over to us?" an officer yelled at me.

"No, I'm dying!" I screamed.

My dad came up behind me, clutching William against him.

And then another officer yelled to my dad, "Sir! Can you take her with you?"

"Come on, Katie," my dad said. "We have to go. You have to get up. Let's go." My 67-year-old dad, also shot and bleeding, picked me up off the ground and brought me to safety behind the police barricade.

I was taken to the hospital by helicopter. My hand was barely attached to my arm, and I had another gunshot wound in my chest. My father and I both underwent surgeries the following day and spent close to one week in the hospital. We shared our physical pain, which kept us pacing at night.

After leaving the hospital, I underwent grueling, year-long occupational therapy sessions and outpatient therapy for PTSD. And in what felt like an instant, I returned to work and tried to be normal. I kept reminding myself to keep my shit together. "Keep it together for your son," I reminded myself daily. But there was only so much I could keep together without shattering.

Being wounded by gun violence is a lifelong curse. I might look OK on the outside, but while writing this piece, three of my five fingers are numb, and I cannot feel the computer keys. No one ever notices how my hand is formed differently than my left. How I'm missing a knuckle. How I lost bone. How my right fingers are shorter than my left. How there is nerve damage and numbness. Nobody can see the bullet scars on my left breast, the one circle on the right, and the one on the left. The circles are where the bullet entered and exited. These bullets just missed my heart.

As for Tom, he spent nearly five years in the county jail awaiting trial. Thankfully no bond was issued. If it had been, he would've finished what he started.

We went to trial in February 2017. The prosecutors were two dynamic women, both ready to put him behind bars for good, while Tom's attorney maintained involuntary intoxication as a reason for the shooting. His attorney claimed that Tom went to the VA hospital that day complaining about depression and anxiety. He was given Klonopin, a benzodiazepine that relieves anxiety, and that he took too much, which caused him to become homicidal. The jury didn't buy it. He was found guilty on all five charges against him, the two most serious being premeditated attempted first-degree murder of my dad and me. Two months later, our judge sentenced him to 60 years in prison, making him 110 years old by the end of his sentence. He'll leave jail in a body bag.

My son William is now 14 years old and in eighth grade. He's an incredible human being who is empathetic, funny, and kind. He was diagnosed with PTSD from childhood trauma, which manifested in severe worry about me. It's gotten better over time, but it's still there. Since he witnessed my shooting at a very tender age, my son realized I could die, which initiated a protector response. He shouldn't have to feel this burden.

As a result of this shooting, I got involved in gun violence prevention and domestic violence awareness. I co-authored a book. I've spoken on the steps of the US Capitol. I've testified before Congress. I've been featured in documentary movies and the media. This was how I chose to fight back against something that never should've happened. But because of this tragedy, I went from powerlessness to empowerment.

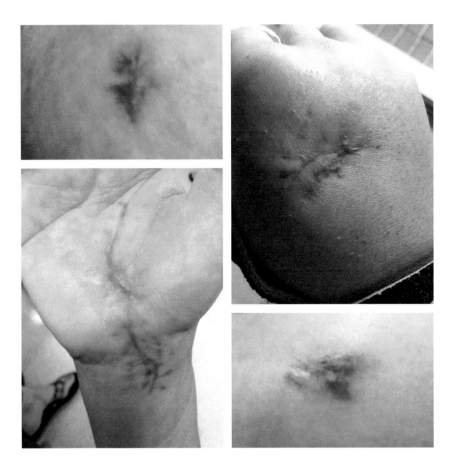

Figure 4.2 The scars Kate bears witness to every day.
Source: Kate Ranta.

Red Flags

ROBERT RANTA

As Kate and I struggled to shut the apartment door against Thomas Maffei's belligerent entry, three hollow-point bullets from his 9mm Beretta exploded, slamming into us. Thankfully he missed his four-year-old son, who stood just behind us. Unaware of still being in the line of fire, my mind scattered like the shrapnel in our bodies.

My left hand shriveled. I looked at Kate, dazed, focusing on her right hand and letting loose bone-chilling screams. *I'm 67 years old and a dead man*, I thought as Tom forced his way into the apartment. He aimed at Kate and pulled the trigger again, sending a second bullet into her left breast.

He'd carefully aimed through the door at our mid-sections because that would do the most damage. He knew this well as a recently retired officer from a career in the military. Later in the melee, he stood over me and trained his weapon, the red laser moving over my prone body. *Here comes the kill shot*, I thought. I refused to look at him. I didn't want him to be satisfied with seeing the fear in my eyes, though my shaking body must have been a tell-tale sign. He shot again, striking me in the chest.

Tom's bullets permanently disabled my left hand. The radial and median nerves are severed forever. I have no feeling in parts of my forearm and three and a half fingers, yet inside those chronically swollen fingers is a discomforting, constant pulsing sensation, pins and needles. Occupational therapy that spanned two years and a third surgery 15 months after the shooting failed to improve the use of the fingers. Because my left hand and arm are shriveled, my body is off balance. I cannot perform everyday life tasks without help, and the absence of full use of my limb complicates other tasks.

Before the shooting, there was no reason to think Tom was capable of trying to kill my daughter, his son, and me. In hindsight, however, there were red flags, including a fast-track courtship followed by a cloistered Vegas marriage, frequent ER trips for an Oxycontin drip, separating himself from others at Ranta family gatherings, and gradually distancing Kate from her friends and us.

Fear and insecurity were our companions. In our driveway one night, Tom slashed a tire on our car and damaged Kate's car, making it undrivable. Later he reimbursed me for the damaged tire, simultaneously admitting his guilt. I found it a coincidence that a tire on Kate's car was slashed after she got home from work to her new apartment on November 2, 2012, just before his appearance, semi-automatic in hand, at the front door of an apartment he was not supposed to know about.

Another time, his commanding officer in Maryland telephoned to tell us that Tom had gone AWOL from the base. He was restricted after the Air Force discovered he'd already been away without official leave, living in Florida the preceding five months while still on active duty, abandoning his military assignment, and collecting his military salary. We all hid for two frightening days at the commander's suggestion. During this time, the military attorneys investigating Tom for fraud and spousal abuse discovered evidence sufficient for a military trial. Still, the commanding officers overrode the Judge Advocate General's court martial recommendation, covering their errors and embarrassment by mustering Tom into retirement, leaving him free to torment Kate, her boys, and our family for the next 17 months.

And then there was more distress when he delayed returning his toddler son William, as agreed, from both Child Protective Services supervised visits and unsupervised visits, repeatedly threatening to abscond with the boy. Or the time when three-year-old William was alone with him on an unsupervised visit and was encouraged to touch and handle a firearm (I wonder now if it was loaded), the same handgun he later fired through the door directly at his son. Or the anguish of being awakened by a phone call from our hysterical daughter after a threatening Tom snatched a sleeping William from his crib, placed the then two-year-old unbelted on his lap behind the steering wheel, and careened recklessly down the road, craftily returning William to his bed just ahead of the sheriff's arrival. William's distraught, frantic mother explained between sobs to law enforcement what had occurred as a cool, calm Tom, the ultimate con-man, charmed police with slick lies about his overly dramatic wife, about injuries suffered in Iraq (where he was never deployed), and gifting officers with military coins. One officer later confessed that the Broward Sheriff's Office (BSO) responders had gone easy on him during this domestic violence call because of Tom's military service. Subsequently, Tom spent a night in the Broward County jail but was released the following day, escalating the paralyzing fear of possible reprisals so much that we sought shelter away from our home again.

There was also the horror of a late-night call about William being rushed to the emergency room after Tom had given his son the adult prescription drug Ambien, claiming to police that William self-ingested one carelessly dropped. Tom's life-threatening actions sent William to the ER and into Florida Child Protective Services. They led to Kate's and our entanglement with a dysfunctional bureaucracy that disregarded William's well-being but fastidiously ensured Tom's parental rights. It placed its scrutiny and suspicion on us, the law-abiding protectors of William, at times threatening to take William from his mother. For unsupervised visits with his son, I met Tom at the local BSO office so often that toddler William began calling the building "Daddy's house."

There was fright when a neighbor in a different apartment complex observed a vehicle fitting the description of Tom's SUV parked in Kate's driveway. Upon her return home, Kate found the slider open and a drawing of a penis on her son's bedroom wall. Or the occasion when Tom, then estranged and in Maryland, texted vacationing Kate saying he had sent a guy into her vacant home. What or who would our daughter and young sons encounter upon their return home? On this occasion, abuser Tom himself had flown to Florida from Maryland and broken into the vacant home with changed locks, the tell-tale sign of his presence being the disappearance of the video surveillance recording equipment. The BSO told Kate that a home-owner could not break into his home.

We witnessed the deepening fear creep across the faces of our son, his wife, a few relatives, and close friends as they realized that connection to our lives could jeopardize theirs.

Over time, the accumulation of the red flags sent me to read about psychopathy and sociopathy, the definitions of which perfectly described Tom. Maffei did not snap. Psychopathic domestic and gun violence abusers are methodical and impassive. At trial, his demeanor was not that of a repentant, self-aware defendant, after four and a half years behind bars, who recognized that his contrived, so-called drug-induced defense placed us in harm's way. We saw a father, husband, and defendant stone-faced, cold, expressing not a scintilla of emotion or feeling or remorse or grief, just an occasional smirk; these indicators suggested depravity, not contrition. Similarly, on November

2, 2012, Tom's actions were unfeeling, dispassionate, and without empathy. His words were coherent while he savored the life-and-death power and control he had regained over his wife at the end of a gun barrel spewing hollow-point bullets, point blank, deliberately chosen for maximum internal damage.

He chose to come to Kate's apartment armed with a death-dealing gun and fire it many times after having read up on strategies for how to kill a wife. He is still the same coward, a bully with a Beretta, who held the three of us hostage. He lined up his extra box of ammunition, knife, rope, flashlight, and handgun on the kitchen counter, hands visibly away from the firearm so entering police did not shoot him in a volley of fire as he done to us. Planned. Methodical. Cool. Calm. Calculated. Psychopath.

I now live with PTSD, including concentration issues, daydream and nightmare flashbacks, and depression. Although these issues are slowly decreasing, I remain under the care of a psychiatrist and, after three rounds of trauma counseling, still schedule sessions with a PTSD-trained therapist as needed. Two of the prescription drugs I take are attributable to Tom's violent, homicidal ambush.

But the mental wounds have had a profound impact. The fear, anger, anxiety, and stress consumed me until April 7, 2017: sentencing day. The struggle to achieve stable mental health took six years. Our daughter's once free-spirited, professionally successful, and debt-free life rapidly declined into an isolated, financially bankrupt, dependent nightmare. She had been pushed from her home to satisfy Tom's psychopathic need to dominate, control and win at all costs. He immediately exerted his abuse the day following their marriage by detailing for Kate, wife four, his plan for killing his third wife; think about the mentally chilling and coercive effect this message sent to newlywed Kate.

Tom has negatively impacted 10 of our 17 retirement years as we supported and protected our daughter and her sons from what we came to understand was Maffei's emotional, psychological, and financial domestic abuse. The Maffei years from 2007 to 2017 were chaotic, disruptive, and irrational. Short- and long-term plans and activities were derailed or canceled to accommodate Kate's, William's, my legal, medical, and psychological needs, and William's school and care demands; moreover, Maffei's financial impact on us stands at a whopping $50,000 debt.

There was light in this blackness, however. Susan, my wife of 53 years, has been the heroic caregiver to three generations of loved ones grappling with a near-death experience. She bandaged, in all ways, our psychic and physical wounds in a whirlwind of loving, selfless devotion. Thanks to Tom, she could not help more in caring for her ailing and dying mother in another state. We believe the unnecessary excessive mental and physical stress of absorbing our pain and holding our family together for four and a half years contributed to Susan's emergency pacemaker implant surgery. We still feel the guilt for the disproportionate time, attention, and money, however necessary, directed to

Kate and her boys at the expense of our son Matthew, his wife and their two young sons, who are also victims of Tom's felonious acts.

Our grandson, William, is the person most impacted and will be throughout his life. Maffei has no financial responsibility for his son because a Florida court order has terminated Maffei's parental rights. Florida is one of only six states that terminates child support under this circumstance. Fewer resources, according to studies, means diminished life opportunities for his son. Maffei has deprived William of a stable, secure, two-parent home. Maffei's actions caused his son's relocation six times in four years. Maffei sent William to trauma therapy at age four. Maffei caused William's PTSD. Maffei brought on extreme anxiety and agitation for William when his mother was out of sight, wanting to protect her, doors always locked, and lights and sounds on throughout the night. Maffei stripped William of his childhood at age four and propelled him into an adult world and adult thoughts beyond his development and language to comprehend. One time, William was reprimanded at school, and at home that evening, he was inconsolable because he thought he was a bad person and was afraid he would be an evil man like Tom.

Nothing gave Tom a license to kill and put his son, his wife, and our family in a position to defend our humanity, worth, and right to live. Knowing that he is jailed and protected from his father has given William the sense of safety he deserves, as it does us. The judge's sentence was 50 years mandatory day for day, plus ten additional years for associated charges. This sentence gives William the best chance to overcome the formidable obstacles Maffei placed in his way and control his own life in peace without worrying about Tom's intrusion. The guilty verdict on all five criminal counts placed Maffei's deserved responsibility for and consequences of his unlawful actions. For us, the ruling marked the point at which we were no longer star witnesses but acknowledged victims from a legal standpoint.

We, forever changed by the near-death experience, have determinedly labored to regain peace and feel joy and gratitude as survivors. At the same time, we raise strong voices for those wounded by domestic and gun violence and the voiceless murdered. We are a stronger family; I am more appreciative of life, my family, and my friends. I have a greater awareness of the centrality of emotions and understand that the struggle to achieve good mental health far exceeds that of physical healing. I have a heightened awareness of family, lovingly supporting each other unconditionally in all experiences, good and bad.

Then, The Call Ended

SUSAN RANTA

I am the wife of Robert Ranta, mother of Katherine Ranta, and grandmother of William Ranta. I was not at the crime scene on November 2, 2012; I was enjoying dinner with my friend and neighbor at a local restaurant. But when I returned home, I got the call that no parent wanted. My husband Rob's frantic voice told me that Thomas (Tom) Maffei had shot him and my daughter, Katherine. He added that I should meet him at North Broward Trauma Center, that he would arrive by ambulance, and that Katherine would be helicoptered there. I knew it must be a severe wound. There was no mention of William. My heart raced. My palms were sweaty. And then, the call ended.

Shaking like a leaf, I called my son, Matthew. I told him the news and asked him to pick me up at my house so we could get to the hospital. He arrived at our home with tears in his eyes and shaking hands. We broke speed limits and ran red lights as we raced to the hospital. I had no idea as to the extent of their injuries or even if this was a life-or-death matter. I had no idea where William, only four years old, might be. I kept telling myself to keep my head together, and stay steady, as my family would depend on me to help them once we were together. En route, I called my daughter's cell phone one more time, and to my intense relief, there was a response. Her friend, who had been at the scene, had also taken her cell phone and told me that he and William were at the police station. He added that a detective was talking with William right then. I replied that he should tell William that his Aunt Lauren, my son's wife, would pick him up and take him to her house, where he would be safe and sound. My relief was profound.

My son and I arrived at the hospital almost on two wheels. The ambulance arrived, and we discovered that my husband was already in the ER. Then we heard the distinctive sound of a helicopter approaching. I looked into the night sky and watched as it flew my wounded daughter towards the helicopter pad. Imagine how frightening that must be. My heart skipped beats.

My son and I were then ushered by hospital staff into the adjacent waiting room. The wait was interminable, but I knew my husband and my daughter needed extensive medical attention before we could see them. A hospital staffer finally told us they would survive. And when we saw them on hospital beds, tubes everywhere, arms encased in thick bandages, the utter shock on their faces was unforgettable. They were shattered and in agonizing pain, but then relief dressed their faces when they saw my son and me. I can't stop thinking about the horror of seeing their bloodied belongings in plastic bags in the doorway, waiting for the forensic specialist to whisk them away for examination.

The doctors and nurses were most accommodating to my son and me, for which we remain grateful. The police stayed to talk with us patiently and firmly. The emergency medical team remained nearby to ensure my husband and daughter would survive. Both needed serious surgery the next morning, and my daughter also needed a blood transfusion. After gently bidding them goodnight, with the assurance that we would return in the morning after surgery, my son and I drove back to his house, though not to sleep a wink after that.

Thomas Maffei may have been an officer in the Air Force, but he is no gentleman. The aftermath and impact of gun and domestic violence upon the victims go unappreciated in American culture. As a family, we experienced that attitude firsthand. After hospitalization, victims face time off from work to recover, time off for doctor's visits, time off to meet with police and lawyers, and time off for trial dates. As a result, victims often lose their jobs, with the added impact of medical insurance termination.

My husband and I are retired educators, so we did not face the above dilemmas. My daughter was extremely fortunate to have an empathetic CEO and manager. In the immediate aftermath, she received her full salary until the New Year. They arranged her schedule to include working two days a week, using the other three days for intense Occupational Therapy for her wounded right hand. The following month, that schedule was flipped to three workdays and two for OT. We all remain forever grateful for their forbearance and their trust in our daughter's work ethic and expertise. And we thank the surgeons and the OT for their competence, care, and concern.

My husband and daughter have regained some use of their arms and hands. Two nerves had been shattered in my husband's left arm above the elbow, and a bone broke in his forearm. The fractured bone healed, but the shattered nerve never regained its vitality. Subsequently, his left arm is limp, hanging by his side, and his left hand remains incapacitated. Daily tasks remain difficult, offering constant reminders of that horrific night. My daughter's right hand remains numb and without the strength to carry out tasks, making kitchen duties particularly challenging. Although she can write with her right hand and hold a fork to eat her food, she has essentially learned to become left-handed. Thomas Maffei has committed a life sentence upon them.

We later learned that Maffei used a military-style gun manufactured to inflict as much bodily damage as possible with hollow-point bullets. His intent was clear; bullet wounds on my husband's and my daughter's bodies were close to their hearts.

No one told Maffei to pull the trigger. He alone inflicted a life sentence on three generations of my family: my husband, my daughter, and my grandson, who is Maffei's only child. The three will live the rest of their lives with the physical and emotional consequences of his actions. Their physical injuries left them with a permanently disabled right hand for my daughter and a disabled left arm for my husband. Every day they see and feel reminders of his betrayal and continually seek counseling and trauma therapy to cope with their emotional and psychological difficulties.

Although William suffered no physical injury, Maffei effectively stole his son's childhood at the tender age of four. Those emotional and psychological scars will run deep. He will need a lifetime of counseling. The Broward Police Department arranged for pediatric mental health services for William to begin immediately, starting the very next day. It continued for the next several days, after which a specialist was assigned to him for weekly mental health services, paid for by the state of Florida. William's preschool worked out a particular curriculum suitable for his needs, for which we are eternally grateful. How special it was to see William stand on the stage with his classmates singing songs for the Christmas and Hanukkah holidays. There was not a dry eye.

As my husband and daughter attest, emotional and psychological scars are excruciating, far beyond the physical pain. As William matures, he will need ongoing mental health services as he grapples with his father's cruelty. Again, Thomas Maffei inflicted a life sentence upon my loved ones.

After a long five-year period, our criminal case against Thomas Maffei began in February 2017. The jury found him guilty as charged with attempted murder in the first degree of my husband and daughter. Young William was not included in those charges because he would have had to take the witness stand. Our prosecutors felt our case was tight enough without his testimony, and given his young age, no one wanted to put him through such agony.

After giving our impact statements to the judge, including William's, he delivered his sentence to Maffei. We all held hands together tightly, waiting for his words. The prosecutors told us to remain silent in the courtroom no matter the judge's decision. The judge sentenced him to 50 years, day after day, to our relief. Other lesser charges made the total sentence 60 years in prison. Florida law does not have a parole stipulation, so that he will serve the rest of his life in prison. Our family will not need to worry or be fearful about a possible release date from prison and possible revenge. We resume our lives a bit shattered and traumatized, but our love sustains us and gives us the strength to carry on to live life with fulfillment. We remain Ranta Strong.

> Clai Lasher-Sommers was shot in the back by her abusive stepfather in 1970 when she was 13 years old and living in rural New Hampshire. Her mother married a man with a temper, who physically assaulted his wife and often promised to shoot his stepdaughter. It finally happened in a bedroom after days of escalating violence. "He used to hold me up against a wall with a gun," says Clai. "And then he would always threaten to shoot me with his gun. Me and my brother." She nearly died of her wounds. More than 50 years later, she's still healing.

Getting Through It

CLAI LASHER-SOMMERS

I spent a lot of my childhood with my grandparents. It was safe and great. The times I spent with my mother were not safe and not great. I lived in a household full of domestic violence and leading up to being shot, there was a lot of violence for two years. It was difficult.

I had a brother who was about 19 months younger than me. My stepfather beat him almost as much as me. It was a horrific way for children to learn about parenting and trust. Early in my childhood, I learned to fight or flee as a result of the obscene amount of torture.

This abuse became embedded in my brain and body, and it's impossible to move past that kind of abuse when you experienced it as a child. That imprint has stayed with me. Sometimes it wreaked havoc; sometimes, it didn't. But that trauma also became passed on to my children. My kids are great, but they had to live with me at times when they didn't understand I had PTSD. I was hypervigilant.

Once I was hospitalized due to a medication error, and I'm glad I was because I learned a lot about PTSD. It created so many issues for me, just like anybody else who has been shot. I lived in rural America, and mental health support didn't exist like it does today, so there wasn't a team of people to help me.

After my stepfather shot me, I was in the best hospital in New Hampshire. But if you read the medical notes, the first thing it says is my name and "allegedly shot." I had almost died. Yet the media it attracted amounted to a small note in the newspaper. My stepfather went to jail for aggravated harassment when he should've gone to prison for attempted murder.

But the story goes further. The night I was shot, my brother was beaten and ran to a neighbor's house, which was quite a distance. The neighbor called the constable. But the constable wouldn't come. My brother walked home in subzero weather, found me shot, and then had to run back to the neighbor's house to get more help. I think this kind of scenario still plays out today. It may not be a careless constable, but it could be a judge refusing to issue a protective order. It could be several things, but it still happens.

I was in the hospital for a long time and remember feeling awful, which I later learned was PTSD. The head nurse at the hospital had no idea how to deal with children who had experienced trauma. It was a complete nightmare. Finally, the hospital sent a medical student to work with me in the afternoons to help me keep up with my schoolwork. Then they sent a psychiatrist to see me before getting discharged. All I remember about that meeting with the psychiatrist was him asking questions and having me take the Rorschach test (looking at inkblots).

After I was discharged, I went to live with my biological dad. He was brilliant but not emotionally available, so it wasn't the best scenario. I ended up in foster care, and then I went to college. Back then, if you were in foster care, staff in the home would put kids into two-year programs. So I went to the University of New Hampshire to study horticulture, and I finished that two-year course before completing my bachelor's degree. When I left for college, I was still waiting for the final surgery to close the holes in my back. It was tough for me to go to college with holes in my back! A few years ago, I returned to get my Master's.

Mine is an endless story of what most survivors go through. It's a story about *getting through it*. But you're left to your own devices if you don't have support.

At one point, I met somebody, and we moved to New York state so that he could get his doctorate. I got pregnant with my first son and met a fantastic doctor. She and I did a lot of work together, including starting a rape crisis center. When you witness that much violence, you know that all is not well in the world, so social justice work and advocacy called me. It was at a time when the US didn't professionalize victim support.

I was the director of a battered women's project in upper New York state, in the rape crisis center, for about 15 years. I think working at the center was good and bad for me. It was good because I was hypervigilant. I could see what might go wrong for the women and children, rise to the occasion, and fight to get them out of horrible situations before something worse happened. But after 15 years, I was burned out, so I started working in construction and ended up on union job sites, doing industrial painting at a time when women weren't on union sites.

Then I met a new partner who became my husband, and we had two children. One of my children now works for the organization Everytown for Gun Safety. She went to college, got her political science degree, worked through elections, and was a great organizer. My son is a builder. There were times my kids had a good childhood. My husband and I didn't have much money, but they were well cared for. We took them on many trips.

We lived in Chatham, near Hudson, NY. My kids, I think, were happy, and then my husband died of lung cancer. His death brought to bear all the grief and loss I experienced as a child. So that was a difficult time.

After my daughter went to college, I moved back to the town of my shooting. I never expected to have horrible PTSD, but I did. I went back to school to get my Master's, and the college building was what used to be the hospital where first responders took me after getting shot.

After completing my Master's, I started speaking out about gun violence, but I had never really needed to do that before because I wasn't around it. I didn't feel compelled. Then a friend who was a lobbyist asked me to speak at an event in New Hampshire, and, after saying no at first, I ended up doing it. And I did it a lot, especially before Hillary Clinton's last campaign, and just continued after that.

Later I got a job in Vermont and was the director of Gun Sense Vermont. I took all my organizing skills and felt like I had a place where I could make a change. When I was there, we passed the first three gun-safety bills to have been given in Vermont.

After that, a job opened at States United to Prevent Gun Violence, and they hired me to be the executive director a month before the COVID-19 pandemic started. I intended to travel across the country to help bring the various survivor groups together and get them into a stronger position in each state (because I don't believe we're going to change things at a federal level for a very long time). I did that job for a year and a half before they ran out of money. However, I discovered working there that once you brought different groups together on the national level, they didn't work well together at all.

There's a lot of ego on the line, so a unified approach to gun safety was hard to come by.

I always look at this gun violence prevention movement and think it needs a redo. In the meantime, what happens is that survivors are not listened to, or they're patronized. I didn't have anyone to mentor me as a survivor either, so, consciously, I've spent the last few months trying to figure out how I feel about totally stepping back from campaigning because I don't think it has been healthy for me. If I ever return to it, I'd have to do it in a survivor-centered way and ensure that there was a lot of support to do it. Without a coordinated path forward, it's difficult to affect change.

The first domestic violence work in the 1980s was all survivor-driven. So were the rape crisis centers. If something is survivor-driven, it becomes very different from what you see now in the gun-control movement. I think we have somewhat of a fractured movement. What is going to help? If we have adequate resources in communities, that will help. But I think we must have a vision that accepts that it's complicated and then move from that space.

As a former librarian, I also believe stories matter, *our stories*. When you pair our stories against policy, maybe that works. But often, it damages the survivor to retell their story repeatedly.

When Everytown began, it looked at people's stories' role in different social justice movements and advocacy, such as the LGBT movement. You take the level of lived experience, and then you build from that. But what is different with the gun-control movement is that there has often been a horrific incident of violence that is too traumatic to relive. Violence will shatter anyone's life; I don't care what kind of violence it is. It breaks you to the core because that's not what we expect from our human experience. That's the part we must take care of within advocacy work because bleeding out your story isn't good for you without significant support. Being a spokesperson takes a lot of bravery, and I don't think all survivors have that.

Notes

1 Warwick Middleton, Adah Sachs and Martin J. Dorahy. *The Abused and the Abuser: Victim-Perpetrator Dynamics*. London: Routledge, 2021.
2 Sandra L. Brown and Jennifer R. Young. *Women Who Love Psychopaths: Inside the Relationships of Inevitable Harm with Narcissists, Sociopaths, and Psychopaths*. Balsam Grove, NC: Mask Publishing, 2018.
3 Patricia Tjaden and Nancy Thoennes. *Extent, Nature, and Consequences of Intimate Partner Violence* (NCJ 181867). Washington, DC: Centers for Disease Control and Prevention. United States Department of Justice, 2000. https://live-cpop.ws.asu.edu/sites/default/files/problems/domestic_violence/PDFs/Tjaden&Thoennes_2000.pdf.

4 Sharon G. Smith, Katherine A. Fowler and Phyllis H. Niolon. "Intimate Partner Homicide and Corollary Victims in 16 States: National Violent Death Reporting System, 2003–2009." *American Journal of Public Health*, 104(3): 461–6, 2014. https://pubmed.ncbi.nlm.nih.gov/24432943/.

5 Martin H. Teicher and Jacqueline A. Samson. "Annual Research Review: Enduring Neurobiological Effects of Childhood Abuse and Neglect." *Journal of Child Psychology and Psychiatry, and Allied Disciplines*, 57(3): 241–66, 2016. https://pubmed.ncbi.nlm.nih.gov/26831814/.

5 Hate Crime

Introduction

What is it like to be a victim of a hate crime at six years old? It's a grim reality when a young child realizes that the adults he depends upon aren't able to keep him safe. How can a child comprehend that someone wants to murder him because of his ethnicity? How is this ugliness integrated into his identity?

These things are so far outside the typical childhood experience that they inevitably change how a youngster moves through the world. There is never an assumption that the world is a safe place.

Even young children experience the fight-flight response.[1] Despite being shot twice and badly injured, little Josh Stepakoff ran for safety on a broken leg. This adrenaline response served him well.

Despite this, Josh and his family were brave. When he was physically able, he returned to the attack scene, which now had added layers of security. Returning to the scene helped him realize that it was still essentially the same place he knew and loved. Returning to the trauma scene under safe circumstances can be a corrective emotional experience that helps some survivors integrate the knowledge psychologically. Ironically, avoidance of reminders of the trauma often intensifies PTSD. With sincere emotional support, exposure can be part of recovery.[2]

A strange social status often comes with surviving an event of extreme violence. It's not the kind of celebrity anyone desires. This celebrity is another layer of complexity that survivors struggle with navigating. It's not helpful when people label shooting survivors as "the kid who survived the shooting."

Josh had tremendous support from family and friends. He put extensive energy into recovery for many years. Because of this, he has integrated what happened and built a happy and satisfying life.

His story is one of hope.

On August 10, 1999, six-year-old Josh Stepakoff had just finished playing a game of capture the flag when a shooter opened fire on his day camp at

DOI: 10.4324/9781003368137-6

the North Valley Jewish Community Center (JCC). He was shot in the leg and hip. The gunman also wounded two other children, a teenage counselor, and an office worker at the center before fatally shooting a letter carrier a few miles away. The shooter serves two consecutive life sentences plus 110 years for multiple convictions. His actions were ruled a federal hate crime.

Just Trying to Be Normal

JOSH STEPAKOFF

At six years old, I became "Josh; the boy shot at the JCC," an identity I would struggle with for my entire childhood.

On August 10, 1999, a neo-Nazi shot me twice: once in my leg and once in my hip.

I had no idea what was happening, but I knew I had to pull myself off the ground and run as fast as possible. At the time, I didn't realize the gunshot broke my leg—or that another bullet was lodged in my hip, only narrowly missing my spine and stomach.

As I ran, my camp counselor stopped me, realizing something was wrong. She picked me up and ran us to the "Little Red School House." Once inside, campers and counselors locked all the doors and hid, waiting for paramedics and police to arrive. I looked around and saw the shock and terror on the faces of all the adults whom I counted for support and guidance. But they couldn't help. They were still processing what was happening, and I realized how devastating this was.

I muttered through my tears, "Call 911."

"We did," the adults said with trembling voices.

I knew that when a regular adult couldn't fix a problem, you call the firefighters, police, and paramedics because they could fix it. After waiting for what seemed like *forever*, police officers carrying rifles walked past the window. Although in pain and terrified, I knew things would get better.

Soon after the first responders arrived, I was loaded onto a gurney and taken to an ambulance for immediate help before transferring to a helicopter to be airlifted to Children's Hospital Los Angeles. At this point, I had begun to calm down. The adrenaline that had helped me to run with a broken leg was now blocking the pain. The flight only seemed like a couple of minutes, and the paramedics kept asking me questions to keep me distracted, like "Who are your parents?", "What do they do?"

I warped the word *epidemiologist* to the medic, which was what my mom was at the time. My father worked for NASA's Jet Propulsion Laboratory, and I was quick to volunteer that information. This communication was before cell phones, so I can only imagine how difficult it was to get this information from me and how difficult it was for my parents to get information about what was happening.

My grandma was down the street from the JCC when the shooting happened. She started knocking on doors, trying to find someone who would let her use their house phone to call my parents to tell them what had happened. My mom raced to the JCC from downtown LA while my dad was glued to the news, trying to get any information he could. With no cell phones, Twitter, Facebook, or any way to get instant news, his decision to stay back was crucial. He found out I was being transported to Children's Hospital Los Angeles and immediately went there. My mom and grandma met at the JCC. My mom remembers the police saying over the bullhorn, "Will the parents of Josh Stepakoff come forward?" It wasn't until then she knew someone had shot me. Authorities then took her and my grandma to the hospital to meet with me.

When we landed at Children's Hospital Los Angeles, my 20-year-long recovery battle began. My cast came off within about six weeks, and I was only on crutches for a little longer. I had minor nerve damage in my leg, which seemed to be it. But as I healed physically, I didn't realize the emotional storm was brewing.

Within a short time, the JCC reopened, and I was back to finish my summer. I did not realize it at the time, but that showed such incredible strength, faith, and courage from my family. It was a very different experience walking up to the JCC that day. A place that had once been open and inviting had changed drastically. Now, you must check in at a guard gate before being allowed in. But, finally, I was back where I felt happiest. Inside, there were some minor changes, but for the most part, it was the same place I knew and loved.

I removed my cast the day before school started, but I still needed crutches as I was relearning how to walk. In the classroom, I got weird looks from my peers, who asked questions about my injuries, which I hated. I didn't know how to answer the questions., Oddly, I didn't like the attention, and some kids revered me for *being shot* as though it were a badge of honor. This return to school was the start of normalcy. At the time, mass shootings were not a common occurrence, especially not ones that targeted kids. Nor were the motives so openly bigoted. The shooting was front-page news, not only across the country but worldwide.

I was excited to see all of my friends, and I wanted it to feel like nothing had changed like we were still rough-and-tumble little kids playing out in the yard. But it wasn't the same. My friends noticed my wounds. I felt isolated and lonely.

Because of my injuries, I sat in the nurse's office during lunch and recess. I was still healing. Although this was purely for my safety and recovery, I felt like an outcast. I was fortunate to have a friend who would come and keep me company, but other than that, I had to pretend I was happy being in the nurse's office rather than being outside playing with my friends like any six-year-old boy should be doing.

At the same time, I was grateful. I had family and friends to keep me company as I healed. All the school's parents knew what had happened to me, and everyone wanted to see if I was OK. Even at six, I was grateful that I had survived and would live to see seven, eight, and nine. Flash forward over 20 years, and I'm healthy and happy. I have a beautiful family: an incredible wife, a daughter, and another child on the way.

Looking back, the people around me and their actions shaped my life and recovery. I spent time, money, and effort trying to cope with my trauma to improve my life, but my recovery is not only the result of my actions; I had help and family. Some survivors don't have this and struggle to heal, move forward, to find healing and happiness. I may be grossly oversimplifying this, but it's something I've discovered for myself: My support system was the backbone of my healing, but it didn't happen without my hard work. With years of traditional therapy, alternative therapy, medication, and determination, I created a life I can be proud of. I worked my ass off. Plain and simple. For years, I had let the shooting dictate my life, identity, and purpose. I was determined to be free from that.

More than two decades after the shooting, I'm a happy, cheerful, successful, and loving husband, father, and son. I have a lot in my life to be grateful for, and I worked incredibly hard to achieve it, to move forward. The most notable of those things has been my recovery. I've spent years correcting, coping, and adapting my life to deal with someone else's decision: to hate with a gun. At the age of six, I had to begin working to overcome my attempted murder and create a new identity that didn't revolve around the shooting. I'm happy to be normal, settled, and at peace today.

Notes

1 "Toxic Stress." Center on the Developing Child at Harvard University, 2020. https://developingchild.harvard.edu/science/key-concepts/toxic-stress/.
2 Elizabeth A. Hembree, Sheila A. M. Rauch and Edna B. Foa. "Beyond the Manual: The Insider's Guide to Prolonged Exposure Therapy for PTSD." *Cognitive and Behavioral Practice*, 10(1): 22–30, 2006. www.sciencedirect.com/science/article/abs/pii/S1077722903800056?via%3Dihub.

6 Mass Shootings

Introduction

It's in our nature to desire a comprehensible linear narrative about our lives, with clear cause and effect to explain the events that occur. It helps us make sense of the world, and when the world makes sense, we believe we know how to avoid danger. But when it comes to mass shootings, the event never makes sense from the victim's perspective.

In this chapter, we read the stories of a reporter at a racial injustice protest, attendees at a music festival, a young woman at a nightclub with friends, a mother, and daughter at a shopping mall, a young man out to a movie, and others simply walking down the street. Some survived but lost loved ones. They have had a variety of ways of coping with their resulting PTSD.

Since these events happen randomly, we all wonder how to stay safe. With the increase in mass shootings in recent decades, it's common for Americans to duck when a car backfires on the street; we look for easy access to exits at concert halls. We scan the crowd in shopping malls, grocery stores, and churches for suspicious-looking people who might be armed. Anxiety disorders in the general population are increasing dramatically, and mass shootings are one reason for this.[1]

Though most of us will never experience a mass shooting directly, we are all affected indirectly every time one occurs. Mass shootings have changed how we move through the world and caused collective reverberations of trauma in our society.

Watching a loved one die is a unique kind of pain. Lives and bodies are shattered instantly, along with their anticipated futures. This kind of pain is a distinct flavor of grief often compounded by survivor's guilt.

There is no "getting over" this kind of loss. No therapeutic template helps someone "move on" after a multilayered heartbreak. There will be no formula for "back to normal" despite the hundreds of books written on the topic.

Many survivors of catastrophic loss describe growing around the grief that becomes a part of them but never growing out of it. Many find advocacy work a meaningful part of their journey.

DOI: 10.4324/9781003368137-7

The best way we can support survivors is to be present with them, listen, attune to their feelings, and never judge their reactions to their experiences.

It's normal to strive to understand catastrophic trauma and, as one survivor says, "in the absence of understanding, to make meaning."

> Ryan Van Velzer is an energy and environment reporter for WFPL News in Louisville, Kentucky. Born in Phoenix, Arizona, he has worked for *The Arizona Republic*, Associated Press, and *The South Florida Sun Sentinel*. Nearly a year after Ryan witnessed a mass shooting, he decided to chronicle the events of that night for an anniversary story.
>
> On May 28, 2020, seven people were shot in a crowd on the steps of Metro Hall in downtown Louisville. No one died, and no one was arrested. Ordinarily, a public mass shooting would have warranted national news coverage, investigations, press conferences, official inquiries, and documentation. But it was only a few months into the COVID-19 pandemic, and that night was the beginning of the city's largest racial justice protests since the Civil Rights era. "The events of May 28 faded from the public's attention amid the most chaotic news cycle of my entire career," Ryan notes. And the invisible wounds remain.

Nine Shots

RYAN VAN VELZER

I'd spent the summer of 2020 embedded with protesters. In between more pressing stories, I'd track down and interview people who had been there that first night. In time, I turned a handful of promising leads into dead ends and disconnected phone numbers.

I placed several records requests, but they weren't much help either. Police wouldn't release the body camera footage. After-action reports concentrated the events of that night into a single paragraph. Incident reports redacted victims' names and were light on details: police found five .45 caliber casings, a bloody shirt, and an abandoned flip-flop.

In the months before the anniversary, I contacted the police seven times for an interview. They declined, instead sharing a brief statement saying they'd welcome any information that could lead to an arrest.

But I caught a break, finding someone who posted a video as the shooting happened. In it, you can hear the sound of a gun cocking, but the shooter remains out of view. I tracked down the man holding the camera and interviewed him. "It was just almost like he was moving his arm back and forth like, tick tock, like a clock arm or something," he told me.

Then I asked if he was OK because I wasn't sure that I was OK.

With the information I could gather, I sat alone in front of a laptop working from home, cobbling together a narrative of what happened that night. Mostly, I listened to my recording of the shooting: dissecting it, staring at the waveforms, counting the shots, rewinding the screams, replaying the seconds until the concussion of a flash-bang [a stun grenade] rings out over the crowd.

The sounds are not so different from the ones that replay in my head to this day. The literature on post-traumatic stress describes this as an "intrusive thought." The literature also tells you that having a sense of agency amid a traumatic event can help minimize long-term impacts.

So, I told myself that I had done my job that night.

In March 2020, Louisville Metro Police shot and killed 26-year-old Breonna Taylor after forcing their way into her apartment. A Minneapolis police officer killed George Floyd on May 25, 2020. The shooting in Louisville happened three nights later, during a civil protest downtown.

The sun was already setting when I received the call from an editor. I was sipping a cocktail during a video-call happy hour with a friend, which was a thing people tried early in the pandemic.

Attorneys working with Taylor's family released a recording of a 911 call made by Taylor's boyfriend, Kenneth Walker. It began in the moments after police had shot and killed Taylor. Walker was terrified, confused, and seemingly unaware that it was the police who had shot his girlfriend or that he had fired at and hit a police officer.

I knew immediately I had to get downtown. I met two colleagues there. It was still early in the pandemic, and we all arrived wearing masks. We carried long, narrow shotgun microphones. Mine had a pistol grip and a fuzzy mic cover.

Hundreds had already amassed in the streets outside Metro Hall when we arrived. They began marching through the streets at twilight. We pursued the crowd, recording every moment: the whipping of the helicopters overhead, the bass of car stereos, sirens wailing past, people shouting. The crowd was agitated and nervous. Loud, sudden noises caused people to scatter. After the second crowd surge, I told myself that I would slow down, look around and think before acting to avoid running blindly in the wrong direction.

A faction of protesters briefly blocked an intersection in front of a bridge over the Ohio River that connected downtown Louisville to Indiana. Police arrived in riot gear carrying long, wooden truncheons and shields to break up the gathering. Demonstrators regrouped outside Metro Hall.

One colleague dropped back to get a broader view of the scene from the steps of the Metro council building. Another colleague and I stepped into the fray. At the street corner, a protester jumped onto a statue of Louis XVI, swung on its outstretched arm, and snapped off the statue's hand.

Riot police formed a line across the street in front of Metro Hall. Some demonstrators threw water bottles. Somewhere in the scrum, police abandoned a transport vehicle on the sidewalk. It looked like an ambulance from afar until you read the words scrawled on the sides. Protesters swiftly took note. They jumped on the hood, slashed the tires, smashed the windows, and began rocking the transport side to side. The entire crowd was in the thrall of the scene: every cell phone, camera, and video recorder in the vicinity was watching and listening.

With the crowd's eyes averted, the shooter opened fire.

Though it seemed like a bad idea, I did it just as planned. I stood still and watched the scene unfold, capturing the sounds with my handheld microphone.

Nine shots. In the recording, they pulse one after another like a metronome. I remember hearing them, but I don't know what I saw. It's an odd gap, in my recollection. I stood staring directly ahead, where I assumed the shots came from, but I didn't remember anything until the screaming began. People ran in every direction. Two trailed behind, limping. A black man fell to the ground in front of me, blood rushing between his hip and groin.

I ran toward him, but within seconds, so did the police. An officer started treating the wounded man. So, I did what I could do: document. I filmed and snapped photos with my phone.

I posted on Twitter. I looked down to check; I had been recording that whole time. My headphones still covered my ears.

The police line pushed up in front of the wounded, forcing us back with riot shields. Sixteen seconds after the last shot, police fired a flash-bang overhead. It was louder than any of the gunshots. Then police began a barrage of tear gas and pepper balls, compounding the confusion until people didn't know if a shooting had happened or if it had been police attempting to disperse the crowd.

I remember snapping a photo of a protester illuminated by a street light and the blue and red flashes of a police vehicle. She held a sign reading, "Who do you call when police murder?"

Figure 6.1 The photo of a protester illuminated by a street light.
Photo credit: Ryan Van Velzer of WFPL News.

A light rain began to fall. I regrouped with my colleagues. I recorded a brief account of what had happened for our station. I drove home, and took calls from family, friends, and bosses. I drank half a bottle of bourbon. I didn't know alcohol can increase the risk of inducing post-traumatic stress.

I took the next day off but returned to work the day after to continue coverage of the protests. Much of downtown was vandalized the night before. Someone had even smashed the windows of the tourism office and stolen the life-sized Colonel Sanders figure from inside. I returned to work early and visited Metro Hall to stare at the scene in the daylight. I wept when I found blood stains where the man had fallen in front of me. Then I went back to work.

A year later, I sat at my desk in my house, mid-pandemic, staring at the aftermath. Through my reporting, I learned that police blamed a protester for the shooting, but they provided no evidence. I interviewed a Black Lives Matter organizer, who said she saw a police officer fire on protesters but had no evidence or other witnesses to corroborate her account. To date, I'm unaware of any footage from that night that identified the shooter.

Still, I wrote what I had. The night before the anniversary story aired, a spokesperson for the mayor called me to say it would be my fault if the city burned down for publishing the eyewitness account of the BLM organizer. We published it anyway. The next day, police reached out to ask for one of my sources so *they* could learn more about the shooting.

I know now that I was writing about the anniversary for myself as much as anyone else. I wanted other people to remember it as I remembered it. I thought it would give me some semblance of control; listening to the recordings would help; if I could gather enough facts, I could make the whole thing make sense.

In the absence of understanding, people search for meaning. I never found it, but I live with that night nonetheless.

Alicia Johnston was shot with an AR15 in her lower back while at the Route 91 Harvest music festival on the Las Vegas Strip in Nevada on October 1, 2017. She survived.

Zach Elmore, a writer and activist, and his sister, Alicia, exchange their personal journal entries below and discover their shared visible and invisible wounds.

Alicia Was Shot

ZACH ELMORE AND ALICIA ELMORE

Journal Entry 1

ZACH'S ENTRY: My phone rang at 10:21 PM. It was my sister, Katelyn. She never called that late, so I knew something was wrong. I answered but couldn't hear anything. She called again and again and again. Each time, my heart sank more and more. Finally, we connected, and I listened to the most horrific thing of my life: Someone shot Alicia in Las Vegas, NV.

My sister, Alicia, and her husband, Nick, had been watching Jason Aldean as he closed out the Route 91 Harvest festival. They thought they heard fireworks, but the man directly next to Nick fell to the ground. He was shot in the neck. They dove to the ground as Nick and Alicia ran for their lives. During a brief pause in the gunfire, they ran again, and a bullet struck Alicia's back.

ALICIA'S ENTRY: There was a burst of popping noises like a strand of firecrackers. I focused on the stage, on Jason Aldean, who was still performing. The man standing beside my husband, Nick, collapsed onto his back. Nick reached down for the man. He tapped on the man's shoulder and asked if he was OK. There was no response, and as he continued trying to bring the man to consciousness, we watched as blood began to pool out from under his head. At this moment, we realized that the noise we heard was not that of firecrackers but gunfire. We were still unsure, but other concertgoers had now begun to cry out in terror, "Gunshots, those were gunshots!"

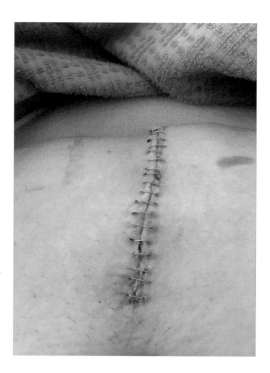

Figure 6.2 Alicia recovering from surgery after suffering a bullet to her back.
Source: Alicia Elmore.

We began looking around us for any sign of what was happening, but all we could see was other people frantically running for their lives. Nick and I took one look at each other and knew we needed to get the hell out of there.

Journal Entry 2

ZACH'S ENTRY: In the chaos, Alicia texted my mom and grandma to tell them she had been shot and asked that they say to her daughters she loved them. We're lucky those weren't her final messages. Fortunately, a stranger with a pickup truck full of wounded people was able to get my sister and Nick to a hospital.

ALICIA'S ENTRY: I'm trying to reflect on the moment I texted my mom, and I'm bothered by the fact that I am unsure of what I said to her. I think I told her bluntly: "There's been a shooting, and I was hit. Please tell the girls that I love them very much." I think the shock had already taken hold of me. This call was between rounds of firing. We had not yet made it out of the concert venue. A couple of ladies crouched beside us as we lay on the ground, telling me to remain calm and that help would come. Then, the stadium lights suddenly lit up the concert venue and us. I remember wiggling my toes and moving my legs; then I told Nick, "We have to move; I can walk. Let's go!" Texting my mom, I had a fleeting thought: *This is it; I'm going to die.*

Adrenaline took over. It was fight or flight now. Nick helped me over the catwalk barriers. There were people all around us trying to get over them. People piled on the ground. I dropped to the ground abruptly on the other side of the barrier. We ran until we were in a clearing next to the stage. There was a cement block and people sitting along it. A man told us to sit there; it would be safe.

As we sat waiting, not sure for what, a group of people carried a man out to the same spot and placed him on the ground in front of us. Nick had been shouting that I was shot and needed help. A woman with a first aid kit came over with some gauze and said to apply pressure to the bleeding while she helped the man. It was chaos, but I could hear them saying he had taken multiple gunshots to his chest. I could see that he was covered in blood and lifeless. I looked at Nick and reassured him that I was doing OK. I knew that I was in better condition than that man.

Journal Entry 3

ZACH'S ENTRY: My mom and I arrived in Las Vegas the next day and went directly to the hospital. The blood-soaked shirt Nick used to stop Alicia's bleeding was in a bag on the floor. Her dried blood was still on his hands. She was motionless in her hospital bed, recovering from surgery to check for organ damage.

ALICIA'S ENTRY: I remember feeling just the tiniest bit of relief as we arrived at the hospital. If they could save me, they would save me.

At the door, Nick was stopped by armed police and told he would have to wait elsewhere. I told him I loved him and walked into the emergency area. There were injured people all around me and blood on the floors and walls.

They put me in a chair in a room to the right of the entrance. A nurse took some vitals and wrote them on my shoulder with a Sharpie. I sat staring at the others and told myself to breathe, to remain conscious. The longer I sat, the more I panicked that I was bleeding out through my bottom. The panic turned to feel like I was going to black out. I told a passing nurse and was moved to the floor so I could not fall from the chair.

Behind me was a couple, both injured. The young woman screamed in pain from a gunshot wound through her forearm. Nurses were moving all around, stepping over me to get to more of the injured. It felt like an eternity as I waited for help. The young woman's boyfriend moved closer to a phone in the corner and offered to make a call for me. I had him call my husband to let him know I was still OK and that I was still alive. I don't remember what I said.

The hospital staff moved me into a room with another survivor suffering from his leg wounds. My adrenaline was wearing off, and the pain was increasing. I started to cry for the first time since the shooting. The man beside me reached out with his blood-covered hand to hold mine. He was trying to comfort me. He had come to Vegas to celebrate his 30th birthday. It wasn't long before the police came in to ask us some questions.

More time passed, and the staff took me for imaging. There were people ahead of me, so hospital beds with waiting patients lined the hallway. I was still crying. I was feeling a lot of pain. Eventually, they did bring me some pain medicine. I remember, too, that this is when I saw my husband again. They had been trying to get loved ones back together.

Once I did imaging, I went to another location to talk with a surgeon. They would perform an endoscopy to check for blood in my rectum. There must have been some, as I underwent abdominal exploratory surgery to inflate my intestines and check for holes.

The next thing I remember was waking up in a recovery room. I think my mom and husband were there waiting for me to wake up. I remember seeing them then. It wasn't until I had made it to my actual room for recovery that I saw my brother. Even in such traumatic times, Zach's sense of humor can lighten the atmosphere for everyone.

Journal Entry 4

ZACH'S ENTRY: The Las Vegas shooter used high-capacity magazines, allowing him to reload less frequently and kill 58 people while wounding hundreds more. The time it takes to reload a weapon can mean the diffe-rence between life and death in a mass shooting. When I campaigned for gun control measures in my state recently, I stated:

"This legislative body has another opportunity to ban high-capacity magazines, which have been used in mass shootings in our state since the last time I testified in support of a ban three years ago. This isn't hypothetical. It happened to my family, has happened in our state, and will happen again. Human life is not acceptable collateral for a bastardized definition of freedom. I urge you to vote Yes on Senate Bill 5078."

ALICIA'S ENTRY: I am so amazed by my brother's work. He is a captivating writer who speaks his mind and heart and gets people to listen and engage in conversation. His empathy and compassion for others go beyond gun control to include women's rights, Black Lives Matter, and many other areas. This activism makes me so very proud to be his sister.

I am much more reserved. While I advocate for stricter gun laws, women's rights to own their bodies, and equal rights for minorities, I am not brave enough to speak out or attend rallies. Still, I went to the cap-ital with my brother here in Washington state to lobby for better gun control and banning bump stocks. I was disappointed in the responses we received from the legislators of my district. One responded that his brother was executed with a gun, but these laws would not save his brother, so the change in the law was not something he could get behind now. I am baffled that this was his mindset rather than focusing on how many lives could be saved.

My husband and I own several guns, and we own a large safe to store them in. I understand the need to protect your home, property, and family. I also understand the importance of being a responsible gun owner. I am not trying to take away anyone's right to bear arms, but the reality is that the Second Amendment was created in a time when owning and using a gun required more than just pulling a trigger. As technology, ease of access, and ease of gun use change, so should the framework of our laws and amendments. Our rights can be protected even if we modify the amendments of our forefathers and align them with the world now. No person should need access to military-grade guns or clips that house more than 10 or 15 rounds.

Mental health is a massive part of the tragedies that have resulted in mass deaths and injuries. Addressing mental health and gun laws together would have a much more significant impact than addressing either alone.

On June 12, 2016, in Orlando, Florida, Patience Murray was held hos-tage for three hours in a bathroom stall at the Pulse nightclub shooting. She was shot in both of her legs.

Mother, Here Are My Wounds Without You

For my mother, Wanda

PATIENCE MURRAY

For so many years, I wallowed in anger towards my mother, Wanda. "What kind of woman would leave her child at two years old?" I often asked myself.

Her absence sent a cold wind to my heart each Mother's Day. Anger consumed me. Teachers forced me to write a Mother's Day card in my third-grade English class. "You can address it to your grandma," my teacher said. It made perfect sense to her, but not to me. I wanted to write to my mother like the other kids. Even then, writing "mother" felt weird and saying "mother" felt wrong. It was a word intentionally left out of my daily vocabulary to avoid the agony that came with each syllable.

I turned to religion to help me heal the emotional wounds left by my mother and the physical wound left by the shooting at the Pulse nightclub. God took me through a transformation inside, opening my eyes to a new way of using my mind. Thinking positively about her absence was another choice on the table. Another life that didn't involve harboring hate toward the very woman who brought me into this world.

I remember reading Deuteronomy 5:16: "Honor your father and your mother, as the LORD your God has commanded you, so that your days may be long and that it may go well with you in the land that the LORD your God is giving you." I struggled with this scripture as a kid. I couldn't see it any other way until God showed me that I *am* my mother, *wounded* like her.

On June 12, 2016, my life changed forever. On this night, I suffered several gunshot wounds during the Pulse nightclub shooting in Orlando, Florida. Like my mother, I was barely hanging on but too proud to ask forgiveness. I feared my wounds shaped me, shamed me. I selfishly self-destructed around the very people who needed me the most. Later I realized my mother is *just* a woman, a wounded woman, like me. While not wounds of the flesh, my mother's wounds run deep like mine.

Like Wanda, I hid my wounds behind an intoxicating smile that could charm the birds from the trees. Too proud to pray for help until I asked God, "What is your dream for me?" I stayed silent, waiting for God to answer. And in that silence, I thought of Pulse. I remembered the throbbing pain of my gunshot wounds and the throbbing pain of watching people die. I asked God to take my soul from my body in those moments. At the time, I thought this was God's dream for me. I was losing hope, giving up on life.

As I continued to sit in silence, I repeated the question, "God, what is your dream for me?" The answer was my mother. The weight of hating the very woman who gave me life lifted. Like my mother, I was alive, but perhaps only one of us survived our wounds and dressed their depth with love and patience. For the first time, I *saw* us both, women before our wounds.

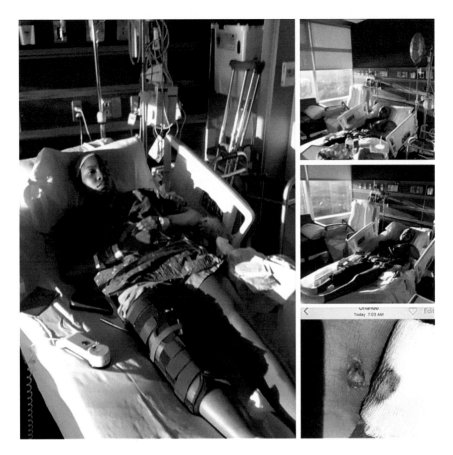

Figure 6.3 Patience in the hospital after the Pulse shooting.
Source: Patience Murray.

For so long, I held on to this notion of not being capable of love or being loved. I believed this to be true for myself. Having these toxic thoughts since childhood resonated deep within my spirit and created a realm of self-hate that consumed me for most of my life. I asked myself, "If my mother left me, who's ever really going to love me?" But someone did, many people. Even in that bathroom stall, someone loved me even as the shooter claimed lives around me. God whispered, "You are here. You can live with scars, even with open mother wounds." I just had to ask, listen, sit in the cold stillness, and open my heart.

But God told me I could release that anger and give it to Him. I gave Him all the tears I cried in my mother's absence. I gave Him my rage and sadness for all the moments I missed with my mother, for all the years she wasn't there to hold me, to watch me grow up, and to be my hope in that bathroom stall, and to give me the will to keep living and loving.

By forgiving my mother, I freed myself from self-hate and the narrative I stitched into the seams of my life that read, "I am unlovable because of my wounds." I realize now my wounds do not affect my capacity to love. My husband, Alex Murray, is evidence of this. The night I was shot, a young woman who came to the club, Akyra Murray, Alex's sister, was tragically killed. Alex and I fell in love in the aftermath of the shooting. Since then, we have produced a three-part docuseries called *Sincerely, Patience* about my experience at Pulse and our lives together, in memory of Alex's sister.

Until God, I didn't realize I was creating a world unrecognizable to my true self. Until God, I didn't know how much life I had to live. And until God, I didn't realize how much love surrounded me, including a community of shooting survivors, Alex, Akyra, and even my mother.

On my wedding day, as I was about to walk down the aisle at the Lincoln Financial Field in Philadelphia, Pennsylvania, the home stadium of the Philadelphia Eagles, my late brother told me, "You look like Mommy." Dressed in my white gown, I cried. She was with me all along. Wanda is me. I am Wanda, fearfully and wonderfully made.

She, my true self, is healed, is whole, and *she* is love. I get to choose the images, meanings, and feelings I have toward my mother. And I choose love. I won't let my mind defeat me anymore or keep the wounds open, bleeding. Instead, I tend to these wounds like a garden. I return to old roots and growing

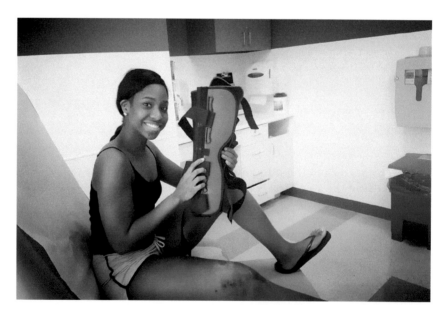

Figure 6.4 Patience in recovery.
Source: Patience Murray.

blooms and listen to the ground's pulsing life. Instead of hating the weeds that have torn through the cedar mulch, I love them too, using them as my compass. They remind me that the world is complicated but not without love, not without God, mothers, women, and wounds. And to love those wounds is to love Wanda, the mother I've never met but the mother who has been with me the whole time, inside my blood, in the wounds that dressed my legs and the breath that kept me going, the breath that whispered through the bathroom stall, "It's not your time, yet. You still have more dreaming to do."

Alayna Buhr is a survivor of the Oregon District of Dayton, Ohio, mass shooting on August 4, 2019. She was having a night out with two of her best friends at Blind Bob's Bar, where she also worked when she heard a loud POP POP POP. She assumed it was fireworks and waited for the light display. But it never came. As the pace in the bar sped up, Alayna knew something was wrong. Her body told her to move. She looked at her friend, who stood frozen. "Run," she yelled. And then they ran. Alayna was shot in the leg by the gunman.

My Body Told Me, *Move*

ALAYNA BUHR

Everything went black. *Why can't I see?*

I panicked. There was burning pain in my thigh when my feet hit the floor. The inside of my leg felt like it was on fire. When I looked down, I saw the hole and the blood pouring out. I covered my wound with my hand and continued running faster toward the staircase at the back of the bar. Working there, I knew I'd be safe if I just got into the administrative office. I ran into the bar after getting shot and yelled at people to run, too. As I was running to the upstairs office, a group of people followed me. Once we all made it upstairs, we barricaded the door.

A few hours later, help came, and officers assisted us down the stairs. I remember asking a few times to confirm these helpers were help, not the shooter playing games with us. When we finally got downstairs, I collapsed into a bar chair. Someone I didn't know made a tourniquet from a belt. All the lights were on in the bar; I'd never seen it so bright.

My friends were alive.

Officers with big guns came in and promised me a stretcher, but the town ran out of ambulances. Instead, my friend helped me get out of the chair, and an officer put me in their car and drove me to the ER. Inside, doctors rushed to cut off my clothes.

"Am I going to die?" I asked the nurse.

Nauseous from nerves, I leaned my head back on the gurney while the staff undressed me.

"I don't know," she said. "We're going to do the best that we can."

After they stabilized me and moved me to a private room, they let me call my mom. I wanted her to know there was a chance I might die. The hospital was locked down. Any visitors needed a password to visit.

After multiple x-rays, surgeons said they couldn't remove the bullet in my leg. The reason is that it missed the bone, and it would do more damage to trying to extract all the bullet fragments. There were so many pieces inside of me. I remember asking the x-ray technician if I could see them.

"Are you sure?" the tech asked.

When I looked, my leg looked like a constellation. Tiny pieces of bullet were scattered everywhere. The doctors said we just had to let the wound heal. So, they sent me home. My husband changed my dressing two times a day. I couldn't do it. It hurt and terrified me.

I was on leave from work for a month and a half. During recovery, I felt like I was in a different world. I wanted to return to work and be around people who understood me. Or at least I thought that was the answer. But when I returned to work, I became disoriented. Everything that was once familiar seemed surreal, like grabbing supplies from the office, patrons asking me questions about beer selections or songs on the jukebox. I tried to power through these feelings but learned through therapy that not all emotions are

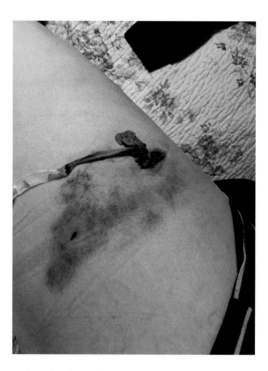

Figure 6.5 Changing the dressing on Alayna's leg.
Source: Alayna Buhr.

meant to be treated this way. I had to find a way to manage my PTSD, live my life, and be a parent to my six-year-old and now new baby. But it's challenging to parent when you are more aware that anyone can shoot and kill the people you love.

My daughter started kindergarten one year after the shooting. I was terrified to send her to school. I even considered getting her a bulletproof backpack, the existence of which saddens me. Each time I send her to school, I worry. I watch her skip down the hallway to her classroom, and a small part of me wonders if it will be the last time I see her. I wonder if I will get *the call*.

I avoid going to the grocery store because they are popular targets for mass shootings. And I don't like going to festivals. I didn't like going to the movie theater before, but I don't go now. I've tried to find a way to balance what I know with reality, so I don't miss out on life. Or let my daughters miss out. But it's hard. I have to navigate these fears every day.

I have a lot of anger about the shooting. I'm angry that I was having a girls' night out, which ended with me shot. I'm angry I was left with $80,000 in medical bills. I'm angry I got shot by an angry man who should've never had access to a gun. And I'm angry that our government is doing nothing to help.

People are numb to gun violence in America. It's easier to accept platitudes than to remain angry and worried. The longer people believe gun violence *is just part of life*, the longer it will be a problem. There's no genuine concern for gun violence or its survivors. But we are all one-angry-man-with-access-to-a-gun away from being shot and traumatized.

I don't see myself as a victim, although technically, I am a *victim*. I associate the word with pity, and I don't want anyone to feel sympathy for me. I did everything I could to survive the shooting. I acted quickly and kept my wits about me. I made a plan. I kept it together. I survived, and that's an accomplishment.

But there is no avoiding trauma. I still remember the smell of smoke and my blood. The first hot summer day always transports me back to that night in the bar, especially when it's dark outside when I walk through the hallway where I once ran to save my life. I'm still processing all of it two and a half years later. I have so much healing to do, and I don't know how to make peace with the idea that people are shot every day, and so was I.

The best I have managed to do is *keep going*. The bar where I work is in a historic neighborhood in the downtown area of my city called the Oregon District. It's a popular nightlife destination, but in addition to that, it's a tight-knit community of service industry people, shop owners, and misfits. The shooting rocked everyone. Even people who weren't there lost friends in the shooting. Shop owners had to review their camera footage. Bartenders had to use towels to bandage bullet holes. People had to scrub blood off the street. I didn't do any interviews right after the shooting. I had dozens of nationwide and local reporters trying to contact me, but I didn't know what to say. I *just* wanted everyone in my community to be OK.

I wish I could support people more. I hope I could be there for more people. I wish I could go to where mass shootings happen and hug survivors and tell them that I don't know if it will be OK, but that it settles. I hope everyone traumatized by this shooting can see me moving on with my life and say, "If Alayna got shot and can keep going then I can too."

> Dion Green's father, Derrick Fudge, died in Dion's arms during the Dayton, Ohio, mass shooting in the Oregon District on August 4, 2019, where nine people were killed, including Dion's father, and 17 others were injured. Dion is the founder/CEO of Flourishing Under Distress Given Encouragement (FUDGE), a 501(c)(3) nonprofit that helps survivors through traumatic experiences with resources and support. In addition to his foundation, gun legislation advocacy service, and gun rally participation, he serves on the board of Felons with a Future in Upturn, Ohio, and numerous other community initiatives and support networks across the country.

Please, Someone, Tell Me How I Get Over *This*

DION GREEN

I held my father in my arms when he took his last breath. He didn't die in a hospice, hospital, or home. My father, Derrick Fudge, was killed on the street near the entrance of the Blind Bob's Bar in the Oregon District of Dayton, Ohio. He died along with nine other people. Ambulances took 27 people to area hospitals.

I couldn't stop sobbing. I wanted my father to live so badly, and he tried to live out my wish, gasping for air and desperately trying to keep his eyes open. I held him as he let go. I was in disbelief that he was gone, just like that. Shot by someone, I didn't know, nor would ever.

After paramedics took my father away, I cried and walked. I walked and cried, stepping over the injured. Stretchers carried the dead. These images haunt me.

After the shooting, I was in a constant state of anger. I stopped taking care of myself and began abusing alcohol. I wanted to forget how my father died. I needed to stop seeing the blood and tears that kept me awake every night. The alcohol intensified my depression and grief, bringing out more emotions like anger. These feelings affected my romantic life too. I didn't want to be intimate with my partner. I didn't even want to be around her because I was in my world, struggling to live my life. I recognize now that I was rude to my child's mother, saying, "I do not need you or no one else. I'm fine by myself." But I know I spoke those words to her not because I didn't care about her but because my wound was wide open.

I feel that this emotional upheaval has made me stronger, like a phoenix rising from the ashes. I continue to push myself vulnerable by speaking about the shooting and sharing my recovery experience with strangers across the country who want to listen. I am OK with being vulnerable because I lost a loved one in a heinous way. People need to see the pain and the grief I go through; they need to see the mental wounds, which are real. They need to understand the wound is open and bleeds every day because I will *never* get another moment with my father.

I know that I am not alone in this uphill battle. There are so many people suffering from trauma who cannot get help or have no clue they're experiencing trauma. So, by experiencing trauma, I have not only been able to share and identify specific traits of trauma but also encourage people to seek the help available to treat their own.

The shooting also made me fight against the state of Ohio and across the country to improve the compensation programs for victims of crime. And, in December 2021, the bill I was fighting for, Ohio Senate Bill 36, was signed into law by the governor. It helps families with burial expenses, provides mental health resources, and addresses many more needs for support that arise when a loved one is lost to gun violence.

The trauma that stemmed from this event will affect families and friends for the rest of their lives. So, from a fellow survivor, please, I ask every one of you who has experienced some form of trauma to speak with a professional and start working on yourself to live again. Remember, after experiencing something so traumatic, we can never be the person we were, but we can rebuild and work toward becoming the person we want to be. Out of my pain came a purpose: helping survivors with their mental health and advocating nationwide. Part of recovery is a failure, but please don't give up; don't let fear of failure keep you from fighting.

Please, don't give up.

> On February 12, 2007, Carolyn Tuft took her 15-year-old daughter Kirsten Hinckley to buy valentines for her friends at Trolley Square, a mall in Salt Lake City, Utah. "Get down, Mom!" was the last thing Carolyn Tuft's daughter Kirsten ever said to her. Carolyn was shot three times herself. The bullet hit her arm and blew out her lung.
>
> After discovering Carolyn dragging herself along the ground to save her daughter, the shooter, a kid in a trench coat holding a pistol grip shotgun, put the barrel to her pelvic bone and shot her again, blowing a hole out of her back the size of a cantaloupe. He then put his shotgun to the side of Kirsten's head and pulled the trigger.
>
> This is Carolyn's letter to Kirsten.

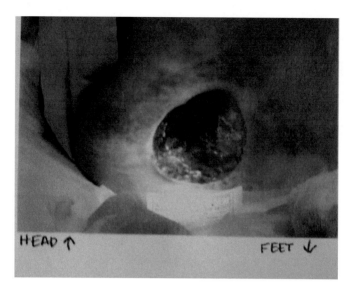

Figure 6.6 One of the gunshot wounds in Carolyn's back.
Source Carolyn Tuft.

My Life Should've Ended With Yours

CAROLYN TUFT

Dear Kirsten, my sweet girl,

It's almost Christmas, and you're not here. You should be.

You should be here baking Christmas cookies and cuddling with me on the couch to watch *Family Stone*. Now, every time I watch that movie, I think of you and how we walked to the theater to watch it, and you loved it!

It makes me cry every time I watch it now. The ending makes me think of you and how many Christmases you've missed and will miss.

You have a gorgeous, blue-eyed, curly-haired (like you) three-year-old nephew, who you'll never hold or teach or laugh with. He will only know you through pictures and stories about his fun and kind Aunt Kirsten.

Every year I pull your ornaments out of the Christmas decorations box and the stocking with your name on it. Suddenly my heart is heavy. Grandma Hinckley knitted that stocking for you. It was supposed to be a treasure to pass down to your kids and to remember her when she was gone. She is still here, and you're not. Every year I see it dangling empty and alone on the fireplace. Scott, Kait, and Parker have all taken their stockings to the homes they live in now.

Figure 6.7 One of the last pictures of Carolyn's daughter Kirsten before she was murdered.

Source: Carolyn Tuft.

I bought a sparkly little, neon-green Christmas tree for you to show people who walk by the cemetery the vibrant person you were, but I haven't been able to bring it to you yet.

My life should've ended with yours, but I was brought back to life by some miracle, and I'm suffering among the living. My body was ripped apart by the thousands of lead pellets, the same ones that ended your life and catapulted mine into hell.

Remember how I constantly said, "Let's go hiking!" and "I'm going for a bike ride"? Besides having you *and* your sister and brothers along, my bike rides were my joy, my reason to get up in the morning. I could never get enough. I was constantly looking for a new trail to hike or ride my bike.

You were so much like me that we both loved adventure. We both loved traveling and meeting new people. We both lived for a new way to create a new and fun memory. We both had a sense of fun mischief, never mean, but a good laugh.

We both had a quirkiness that other people somehow found endearing. Go figure. Ha!

Everyone loved you. You loved everyone. Your kind, compassionate heart, and tender soul made it easy for people to laugh and cry with you. You were a confidante to so many friends and to me!

Your life ended so abruptly that it leaves a gap, a massive void in my heart and life. A bullet took you mid-sentence, and we will never know what the rest of that thought could have become.

It's NOT OK that anyone can buy a gun in the US just as quickly as a gallon of milk.

It's NOT OK that someone can carry a gun into a store where moms take their daughters to buy valentines and take their lives away within seconds.

It's NOT OK that a stranger with a gun, who is having a bad day, can take away all your dreams and aspirations.

It's NOT OK that someone, because of lax gun laws, can easily purchase guns and take away the life of a beautiful child from a mom who spent 15 years loving, shaping, caring for, worrying over, crying for, laughing with, cooking healthy food for, helping prepare for the future, and having conversations about the future with, conversations about when she will have children of her own and being excited about it, preparing for learning to

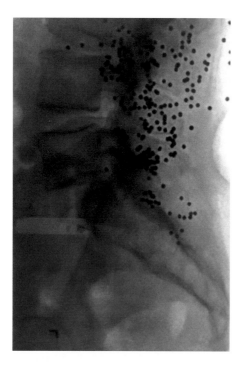

Figure 6.8 The pellets in Carolyn's lungs and back.
Source: Carolyn Tuft.

drive and go to the prom, and the college she wants to go to become an architect like Frank Lloyd Wright.

It's NOT OK that someone can take that away so easily.

It's NOT OK that I lost EVERYTHING that day. I lost my business, house, health, security, and ability to work and provide a living for myself and my three other kids.

It's NOT OK that every day since February 12, 2007, I have lived in constant pain and sickness from lead poisoning and missing body parts. I now live below the poverty line and pay the consequences for some stranger with a gun.

I badly need to talk to you.

Mom

> On October 1, 2017, a man opened fire on the crowd attending the Route 91 Harvest music festival on the Las Vegas Strip in Nevada. Perched from his 32nd-floor hotel room, the gunman murdered 58 people and wounded hundreds more. Two additional victims died in 2019 and 2020. Emily Cantrell was attending the festival for the third year in a row. The night of the shooting, Emily was near the stage as Jason Aldean performed, and the gunman opened fire. She writes, "A bullet never entered my body the night of October 1, but at times I feel like I have one in my head and in my heart." Emily alludes to the invisible wounds gun violence survivors endure and how those wounds manifested as what she now understands is "survivor's guilt."

Time Will Never Heal All Wounds

EMILY CANTRELL

Whoever helped coin the phrase "time heals all wounds" never understood the invisible pain a bullet can cause. This proverb dates back to ancient times before guns existed. Before children were killed in schools. Before shoppers were killed in malls. Before music lovers were killed at concerts.

I nearly became one of those music lovers killed on October 1, 2017, when I found myself in the middle of what would become our country's deadliest mass shooting. It was one of my favorite weekends of the year and my third time attending the three-day Route 91 Harvest festival in Las Vegas. On the final night of the concert, headliner Jason Aldean took the stage. And at 10:05 PM, my life forever changed.

In ten minutes, a lone gunman used an arsenal of weapons, 12 of which were AR15s equipped with 100-round magazines, to spray more than 1,000 bullets into the concert crowd. At two different times, I thought I was shot. Once, a bullet whizzed through my hair. The second time, I thought I was shot in my hand. It was a sickening matter of millimeters. I stopped running and was ready to give up when a stranger said we would count to three and run together. Somehow, we survived with only superficial wounds. In the end, the gunman shot more than 500 people, killing 58 of them (this fatality number does not include the shooter or those who have since died). The other 22,000 of us survived, but for some of us, the terror never ended.

A bullet never entered my body the night of October 1, but at times I feel like I have one in my head and my heart. I suffer from what I now understand is survivor's guilt. When I arrived home in Seattle the day after the shooting, I received an outpouring of support from people who said how happy they were that I was "OK" and "safe." Little did they know, or did they understand that I was neither.

I watched *Monday Night Football* with friends the first night after the shooting. I remember sitting on the couch holding a beer and looking down at my scraped knees. I started crying as I felt guilty about trying to enjoy the company of friends when 58 others never returned home.

I cried when my physical wounds healed, wondering why I wasn't healing emotionally. I was angry. As the rest of the world moved on, I attempted to deal with the aftermath. The following month, at a Friendsgiving celebration, sounds of laughter from both adults and children filled the kitchen and living room. I stepped outside and burst into tears as I thought about my parents, who may never understand how close they were to burying me.

For months, I slept fully clothed with shoes next to my bed if I needed to run. I feared every night a shooter would break into my home. The only thing that helped was moving into a secure condo building.

The following spring, Opening Day for the Seattle Mariners finally rolled around. The official start of baseball season has always been one of my favorite days of the year. However, this year was different. I did not anticipate that the celebratory sound of fireworks would take me back to that horrific night. Shockwaves went through my chest, and I dropped to the ground, cowering and crying. It seemed the fireworks were never going to end.

While the rest of the world had moved on, the shooting victims were left picking up the pieces. I was trying to find a therapist and learning how to make up for lost time at work. I was trying to figure out how to pay for what would soon become all these unexpected medical bills that insurance would not cover.

To this day, I suffer from PTSD. I am anxious and irritable. I have concentration issues—a lack of trust. I always avoid having my back to the door, and my head is constantly swiveling. Whenever I enter a room, I look for a place to hide and plan an escape route, should I need one. The sound of jackhammering or a car backfiring still makes me jump today.

I have lost friendships with people who don't understand why I can't "just get over it." But the sad truth is that the life cycle of a bullet never ends. Physical wounds often heal, but invisible wounds do not. And for that reason, they can be even more dangerous than a physical wound.

My story is just one of 22,000 that came out of Las Vegas that night. I cannot comprehend how the United States has allowed mass shootings to become normal when there is absolutely nothing ordinary about them. While some people may move on after a tragic shooting, there are countless individuals whose lives will never be the same, simply because time does not heal all wounds.

> In 2012, Joshua Nowlan threw himself in front of gunfire during a screening of the movie *The Dark Knight Rises*. While he survived the mass shooting, Joshua suffered multiple gunshot wounds that destroyed most of the muscle, tendon, and soft tissue in his left leg and right arm. He spent hundreds of hours in countless surgeries and physical therapy, which ultimately led him to decide to have his leg amputated below the knee. Mentally, it's been a marathon recovery. Joshua is a US Navy veteran and single father of two boys.

Is There an End?

JOSHUA NOWLAN

It's a marathon. The finish line is far away—continuous slow motion.

The first 12 months after getting shot were physically and mentally grueling. I had to walk around with a cane and a boot on my left leg, and I had a huge cast on my right arm.

I was extremely self-conscious, constantly worrying if people could see my scars, both a result of the shooting and the series of surgeries that followed it. I worried even more as a single guy, too, thinking that no girl would ever want to date somebody who looks like me because I have all these hideous scars. These thoughts plagued my days and nights. Who would like to be with me?

But the physical aspect wasn't my only worry. There was the emotional impact of being part of a mass shooting considered the largest of its kind in history at that time. I wondered if it was possible to be OK, and I worried I'd be damaged my whole life. I feared what people would be more struck by: the historical significance of the shooting or its effect on me, Joshua.

I wondered how people would react to something like that. Often they ask about how I felt during the shooting, if I'm still in pain, or if I have any advice about surviving a shooting. The list of questions is enormous and sometimes, yes, *painful*.

The first 12 months after the shooting was rough, especially as a single dad with two kids. My boys were doing things they shouldn't be doing as kids. They were helping clean up around the house. They were helping me do my laundry. They even had to cut my food because I couldn't hold a knife in my hand. They had to grow up a little bit faster than they should have. I wrestled with thoughts like: *How are these kids taking care of me when it's supposed to be the opposite? It's my job to take care of them.* I was taking pain pills every day just to get through the day. I wasn't as outgoing as usual. I had a hard time connecting with my friends and other people or attending social events, like parties with friends or family outings. I felt disconnected and no longer craved or welcomed companionship. And even the thought of leaving my bubble created anxiety. I didn't want to go through those long-winded questions that brought me back to the night of the shooting. I became a recluse; it seemed like the only option to avoid additional pain.

I began to realize I wasn't the person I was before the shooting. I knew I needed help but didn't know how to get it. Luckily, my friends and family offered guidance. They wouldn't let me spiral and take my two kids with me. And at the time, I was their sole caregiver. One day, one of my good friends over for lunch called me, "Dude, you need to buck up. You need to see somebody. This is not you." He called me out, and I broke down. "I'll do anything. Just tell me what I have to do," I said.

Shortly after that talk, I was referred to a professional psychologist through a Victims Advocate, whose focus is supporting trauma victims and those suffering PTSD. At first, I tried to be open-minded and tell myself, "They're here to help." At first, I never really believed in counseling. I thought it involved somebody sitting there, nodding their head, asking me, "Tell me how that made you feel," and just jotting down notes on paper.

But after meeting with the psychologist, I realized I had been wrong. He knew what he was talking about because I felt it in my bones. He put me at ease by NOT asking me, "How did your shooting make you feel?"

Instead, we talked about emotional regulation and ways I could manage my PTSD. He told me about how PTSD affects the chemicals in my body and brain. Most importantly, he provided me with strategies to implement when my PTSD symptoms go into overdrive. These strategies were a massive help for me in regaining control of my life.

One of the first strategies I used to manage my PTSD was at the trial after the shooting. While I was sitting in court, I remember an attorney talking about how mass shootings are not an everyday occurrence. Of course, once he said that, the judge made a comment: "If you haven't read the news yet, there has been another mass shooting that just happened."

I almost jumped out of my seat. *Wait a minute*, I thought. The worry and anxiety swirled in my head. *Another mass shooting just happened?* And then, just like that, I was back in the movie theater. I could hear the screaming and yelling. I could feel the bullets all over again, and all at once, inside me.

So, I focused on a strategy my psychologist shared with me during one of our initial sessions. "When you start feeling like you are either back at the shooting or transported to another reality," he said, "the first step is to touch things that you know are physically real around you." He continued, "Once you start touching things, tell yourself what you're touching."

And that's what I did. I started touching the chair I was sitting in and quietly mouthed "chair." Next, I felt the table in front of me and mouthed, "table." I gave names to everything I felt to welcome me back to reality. I told myself, "I see windows. I see walls. I see the person in front of me."

Then I remembered the breathing exercise he showed me. "Start taking slow-moving breaths through your nose and out through your mouth," he said. "And then count back from ten. Count from one to ten or back from ten, whatever's most comfortable for you." Those breathing steps helped to control and reel me back to reality, the present.

I have to walk around with a cane. In my right arm, I have this huge scar. I'm constantly in pain. To me, there isn't a finish line where the pain will stop. That also applies to my mental distress. There will always be movies. Anytime a new film comes out, especially Batman movies, my mind goes right back to the shooting. The race goes on; personally, the finish line is always a little bit further ahead. Each time I get closer to that finish line, it is progress: I am doing something to better myself. Even though the line is still out of reach, I'm doing something for my recovery. I am now doing more of the things that I enjoy. I love being outdoors. I love hiking. I love camping. I love going for runs. I love outdoor activities, like paddle boarding and going out in the water. All those aspects give me a sense of joy.

A significant turning point in my recovery happened in a grocery store. I was picking up groceries and walking to the checkout aisle when I looked at a stack of magazines. On the cover of *Men's Health* magazine was a man with a missing arm and leg. The man in the magazine, Noah, is a veteran who lost his arm and leg serving his country. And then I read about everything he has done to get to where he's at, including *Dancing with the Stars*. He talks about his experience, what he wants, and his goals. At that moment, I felt inspired by his story.

Intimated by physical activity, I started to get back into shape with CrossFit. The trainer, Roger, encouraged and motivated me to keep going. He took the time to help me out, so he's essential in my life.

But, of course, there's the mental aspect because people are still staring at me and asking me to explain my story. I mean, that takes a toll. I had to ensure I knew how to confront the ghosts haunting me, so I returned to the movie theater with my wounds—the place where he shot me and killed and wounded others.

I needed to confront my feelings about where I nearly lost my life. My attorney worked out a time for me to go back to the movie theater and sit in the same place where I thought I would lose my life and face those demons. I mean, that was the biggest mental hurdle. I never thought I would be able to do it, but I was able to. Confronting those ghosts in the place I nearly lost my life, I thought, *I didn't lose my life. I beat you. I'm still here. It's time to move. It's time to move on.*

That's what I did.

Once I started building up that confidence in my prosthetic and myself again, I reached the point where I am today. I would say I'm happier than I've ever been. I'm doing more physical things with my kids. I'm more there for my kids than I ever was. I'm also with a woman who supports and loves me, regardless of my scars and backstory. She accepts it.

I can now see myself using my story to help other people. Now I'm more confident in myself; I can use this story to help other people to bring their confidence up as well so that they can realize it's not over. It's not over, and it will *never* be over. But we will build ourselves up and be stronger people because we're not going to allow our circumstances to dictate how we are supposed to live.

Note

1 Arash Javanbakht. "Mass Shootings Leave behind Collective Despair, Anguish and Trauma at Many Societal Levels." Anxiety and Depression Association of America, May 31, 2022. https://adaa.org/learn-from-us/from-the-experts/blog-posts/consumer/mass-shootings-leave-behind-collective-despair.

7 Random Open Fire

Introduction

A random shooting on the street. An untraceable ghost gun. The story of yet another attack makes no sense and changes the trajectory of a life.

Vincent Gazzani owes his life to two passers-by who rushed to help rather than running away. Vincent is another survivor who has found meaning and purpose in activism, in this case, the fight to get ghost guns banned. Though working out emotional pain can be confusing for someone viewed as a masculine "tough guy," Vincent has found relief through action, using his scars as a personal reminder that he must prevent future shootings.

For Vincent, like other survivors, family support has been vital.

Many survivors experience repeated violations of their boundaries as they recover, from intrusive news media to insensitive friends and coworkers. Survivors may be asked to recount the attack details or show their scars to coworkers. This kind of insensitivity can cause the survivor to experience distressing emotional flooding, which is counterproductive. The survivor must be allowed to determine what aspects of the story they are comfortable sharing and the circumstances around such sharing. After a shooting injury, survivors need a sense of agency and control over what happens in their life. Agency helps increase psychological stability in the aftermath of trauma.

When perpetrators go to trial, it is stressful for survivors as they testify and confront their attacker in court. Some may find that PTSD symptoms intensify in response to this. They may even feel they are losing gains they have made in recovery and need extra support to get through it. However, a trial also offers an opportunity for some degree of closure that can ultimately be helpful.

On April 22, 2021, police officers ran through the Gaslamp Quarter in San Diego, California, responding to reports of an active shooter. A gunman had just shot and killed a valet worker and hurt four others in downtown San Diego, including Vincent Gazzani, a New Jersey native visiting from out of town with three of his friends. Vincent recalls that

DOI: 10.4324/9781003368137-8

the shooter appeared in a lousy mood and witnessed police chasing the man. As the shooter passed by Vincent and his friends, he said, "You guys having a good time?" He pulled out a gun and fired. The shooter was chased and tackled by two people who held him for the police.

The gunman used a homemade 9mm "ghost gun," unregistered. He had a prior arrest in 2017 for resisting an officer and carrying a concealed gun while working as a security guard at a restaurant in the Gaslamp Quarter. In 2019, he pleaded guilty to the misdemeanor of carrying a concealed firearm; court records indicated he had to surrender the gun. KFMB-TV reported an active warrant for his arrest for working as an unlicensed security guard.

Just a Regular Vacation

VINCENT GAZZANI

The word *scar* does not merely refer to something physical. It can be emotional; it can be whatever. My scars remind me of the shooting and that life is out of my control. My scar is not something that's going to go away; it's something that's with me forever. While the word *wound* suggests the present—something that needs to be treated for you to survive—a scar is a mark of the past and yet something ever-present.

On April 22, 2021, my friends and I were in San Diego for vacation. We were in a downtown area called the Gaslamp Quarter, which is not mainly known to be a violent area. We were on our way back to our hotel, pizza in hand, and looking forward to playing golf the next day, when we saw a man wearing black clothing who appeared to be upset and was running from police officers. We were on a narrow sidewalk, and the man ran past us screaming, "Get out of the way," so we did. Within seconds, we heard a bunch of gunshots. And that's when I realized I had been hit: once in the arm and once through the chest.

The shooter had used a "ghost gun," a gun you can assemble using kits or parts purchased online. It's legal to get these parts and make the gun yourself without adding any identifying serial number that can link it back to you. There's no background check, no nothing. You only need a credit card and a shipping address to get gun parts from online distributors.

After being shot, I couldn't breathe or think straight. I was in shock, in between conscious and unconscious. It felt like I got hit hard and couldn't catch my breath. Miraculously, two Israeli ex-officers, Shai and Dvir, who also happened to be in San Diego on vacation, came to my rescue. While most people ran away, Shai and Dvir ran toward me, rushing to dress my wounds. They pressed on my wounds to stop the bleeding and coordinated with my friends to call for help. They got the EMTs there within a couple of minutes. If it wasn't for the two Israelis and the EMTs who came to my aid, I don't think I'd be here right now.

Figure 7.1 Vincent "Vinny" Gazzani (middle) reunited with his heroes a few weeks after the shooting.

Source: Vincent Gazzani.

But once the EMTs arrived, they jumped in to help. I was only conscious for a short time after they placed me in the ambulance and drove me to the hospital. Once in the hospital, I had an emergency splenectomy to remove my wounded spleen. Surgeons also had to repair my stomach and lung since the bullet went through both organs. Doctors had to repair my lung to allow it to return to total breathing capacity. (About a year later, I'm in almost peak physical shape. The medical staff at UCSD did a fantastic job, and my good physical condition allowed my body to heal quickly.)

I was in the hospital for about a week before I could go home. I couldn't fly home because my doctors were worried about how my lungs would react to the altitude. Doctors gave me a choice: either wait a month in California for the all-clear or drive home. I wasn't in good shape at all. I had painful wounds, no core strength, and I couldn't walk. I couldn't do anything. So I chose the drive home. My parents, who flew out to California immediately following the shooting, were with me and didn't want to leave me, so they rented an RV and tried to make the ride home as comfortable as possible.

It was a long trip, taking about five days, with 12 to 14 hours of driving daily. We cut through California, down to Texas, some of the Midwest, on to Pennsylvania, and then to New Jersey. I made the most of the journey with my optimistic nature. Instead of focusing on the negative, I distracted myself by looking out the window at the changing landscape. Eventually, I could get up, walk around, and do my breathing exercises. We stopped at a couple of hotels at night so that I would be comfortable—able to stretch out rather than being cramped in the RV.

Once I got home to New Jersey, I went straight to the hospital to get all my staples and sutures removed from the wounds. I was with my parents and loved ones for about a month until I could get back on my feet and get back to work.

Within a month, I could work from a hospital bed in my home. I'm dedicated to my work, so when customers call me and ask, I will not deny them quotes, bids, and orders. So, I was working pretty much full-time from home. My company knew about my situation, but I didn't know if all my customers did. Some of them still don't know everything that happened to me. But it was good to distract me from work.

I'm in the construction industry, a more masculine industry where many people don't always understand personal boundaries. My coworkers considered me tough and asked me a million questions that sometimes didn't sit well with me. They wanted to see my scars and hear about my injuries. It felt like an experiment. I felt like I was revisiting something that I didn't want to review repeatedly and on demand. I'm not ashamed of the story of my shooting by any means, but sometimes their questions like, "How did it happen?" and "How do you feel now?" are hard to answer in a few words.

I don't want anyone else to get shot when I look at my scars. My experience fuels me with the energy to do more advocacy and charity work. My scars bring out a lot of emotions. It's not pleasant. The scars are a reminder of what needs to be done to ensure this situation doesn't happen to anybody else.

I hope my experience clarifies why we need to ban ghost guns. The distribution of these gun parts should all require background checks and be traceable to the buyer. Otherwise, we face the worst possibility—that a gun ends up in the wrong hands.

8   School Shootings

Introduction

Until recent history, parents sent their children to school every day, assuming that school was safe. This type of safety is no longer true in the United States.

School shootings have occurred in elementary schools, high schools, community colleges, and universities, and an entire generation has grown up under the threat of being murdered in their classrooms. Lockdown drills are now a routine part of the school experience, and this alone is a practice that causes anxiety for students and teachers. The threat of violence changes a child's perception of safety in the world.[1]

The school shooter has become the modern boogeyman, a murderous monster appearing out of the ether with no forewarning to kill children and young people as they sit at their desks. This boogeyman is every parent's worst nightmare.

And as Patrick Korellis shares, each new attack brings a revisiting of a survivor's trauma response. The mind and body respond as if they are once again under attack. There may be an acute experience of threat, sensations of lingering wounds, and awareness of bullet fragments left in the body. These perceptions and intense feelings are startling but entirely understandable. They fuel Patrick's empathy.

Patrick's story underscores the power of survivors reaching out to other survivors in the immediate and long-term aftermath of a shooting. He makes a concerted effort to connect with other survivors in online support groups and in person and has helped pave the way to recovery for countless other survivors. Attack anniversary dates can be challenging, and gathering with other survivors at memorial events can be immensely soothing.

The community has tremendous healing power in feeling understood in ways only other survivors can. Patrick gives us another example of a survivor using his scars to help others heal.

> On February 14, 2008, Patrick Korellis was sitting in a lecture hall at Northern Illinois University, learning about ocean currents in his geology class, when a man wearing a long trench coat kicked the stage

DOI: 10.4324/9781003368137-9

door open, pulled out a shotgun, and started shooting. Patrick hid under his desk. While the shooter reloaded, Patrick ran for the door. He was shot in the back of his head and his arm. Five of his classmates were killed that day, and 21 were injured. "I realized that Valentine's Day would never be the same to me again," Patrick says.

Within a few weeks after the shooting, he received letters from Virginia Tech survivors, who had experienced their shooting just ten months prior. Patrick visited the Virginia Tech campus for their one-year remembrance service. He met with survivors, who told him to expect a long recovery but to lean on his support system, including other survivors. Patrick is part of a private Facebook group for mass shooting victims that a Columbine-shooting survivor started. The group provides survivors with a space to talk, reflect, and support one another.

Fragments

PATRICK KORELLIS

On February 14, 2018, I was back at the Northern Illinois University (NIU) campus for the ten-year memorial of the shooting.

I was in a room with 50 others, all families of the victims and survivors of the classroom shooting. We were preparing to lay wreaths for my classmates when news broke about a shooting at a high school in Florida. I looked at my phone in awe. How could there be another shooting on the day of NIU's shooting remembrance? There was.

Figure 8.1 Patrick at the NIU memorial.
Source: Patrick Korellis.

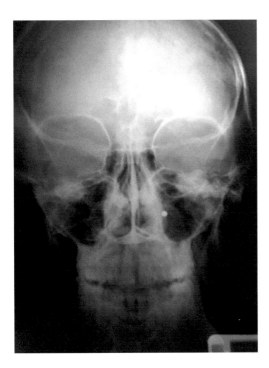

Figure 8.2 X-ray of the shotgun pellet still in the back of Patrick's head.
Source: Patrick Korellis.

I was angry. The bullets still lodged in my bones shuddered. Memories began to flood within me, maybe even fragments of bullets. I felt the bones inside me shift and move. Where were they going? I felt as if the shooting was happening all over again. My palms were sweaty, and my throat felt coarse and hardened.

It's happening again. And again. And again. I gasped. Sobbed. What else could I do? Maybe run? Run to help those victims in Florida? Instead, I felt helpless. I couldn't do anything. At least right then and there.

I felt the bullet in my arm. The small pellet lodged in the bone. I ran my hand over my shirt, which covered my scars. I hugged myself. I imagined I was hugging those kids in Florida. How awful, sad, and outrageous they must run out of school for their lives.

It has been a long road since Sandy Hook, Orlando, Vegas, and Parkland. I've reached out to victims of these shootings and introduced them to the Facebook group.

Parkland hit me hardest, considering it happened ten years after the NIU shooting.

I am so proud of the students speaking out and making a change.

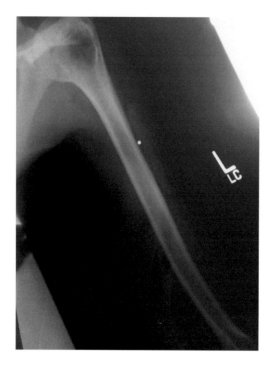

Figure 8.3 X-ray of the shotgun pellet still in Patrick's arm.
Source: Patrick Korellis.

I stand with them 100 percent and am doing the same here in Illinois.

I hope to show the bullets in my bones to those who don't believe they could ever get shot.

I feel like a fragment, a bone fragment. I was once whole, with no holes. Now, I have marks. Now I have small balls of metal inside me to hold like a memory, a bowl of fragments and bullets to remind me this life is mine and that I am still here—and that others aren't. I hope these bones can show the world that everyone is in danger, whether they know it or not. Their bones are placeholders for the bullets I hope they never meet or know.

Note

1 Elizabeth Williamson. "When Active-Shooter Drills Scare the Children They Hope to Protect." *The New York Times*, September 4, 2019. www.nytimes. com/2019/09/04/us/politics/active-shooter-drills-schools.html.

9 Support Resources for Survivors, Their Loved Ones and Advocates*

Despite their different experiences, there are common themes in the stories of gun violence survivors. The shooting becomes a clear line of demarcation in their lives. There is the life "before" followed by the life "after." Everything changed in multiple ways in one moment and will never be the same.

Grief and loss can be overwhelming. The sense of being safe in the world diminishes. Psychological symptoms linger, sometimes for years. Physical pain and disabilities can be ongoing. However, none of this bodes hopelessness. Despite these things, healing happens.

Though the pain is never erased, it's possible to grow around the wound as it becomes integrated into the tapestry of life. We are all more than our traumas.

It's in our nature to move toward healing; it's characteristic that survivors heal by supporting others who have had similar traumas. Helping other survivors often become a life mission, and working as an advocate to prevent gun violence provides a sense of purpose and ultimately saves lives.

Another common theme among survivors is that supporting family and friends is integral to healing. No one heals in isolation. From the event's immediate aftermath to years of ongoing recovery, human relationships have everything to do with how victims become survivors.

Though all survivors experience acute stress, not all go on to develop PTSD; we can view trauma responses on a continuum that is unique to every person. Trauma also ripples outward. Loved ones, helpers, and advocates can develop vicarious trauma in response. Anyone closely involved with a survivor of gun violence may be affected. They are also in need of supportive services.

The following chapter offers "Crisis Support" and "Ongoing Care" resources for survivors, their loved ones, and advocates.

Crisis Support: The Immediate Aftermath

The immediate aftermath of a violent assault can be chaotic and overwhelming for the survivor and their loved ones. They may experience:

DOI: 10.4324/9781003368137-10

- severe anxiety and panic
- tearfulness or shaking
- disorientation and confusion
- shortness of breath
- sleep disturbance, insomnia, and nightmares
- irritability
- survivor guilt

Psychological support is typically minimal or entirely lacking within our current piecemeal healthcare system.

In addition to emergency medical care, other costs like lost wages and continuing medical care are a reality for survivors of gun violence. For example, there may be children to care for and rent to pay. In the aftermath of trauma, survivors and their family must navigate a maze of complex problems when stress limits their executive functioning. Crisis assistance is crucial.

The federal government has funded services for crime victims, which they access through the Office of Victims of Crime and the 988 Crisis Lifeline program. Besides providing immediate crisis support, both agencies can help connect survivors and loved ones to available local resources. Here are a few more crisis support resources with contact details:

> **Office of Victims of Crime:** The federal government provides funding to support crime victim assistance and resources to victims of violent crime. Survivors may be eligible for crime victim compensation benefits, including reimbursement for medical care, lost wages, mental health counseling, and other associated expenses. These services can be accessed locally and are available in every state and US territory. Survivors may contact the VictimConnect Resource Center (VCRC) on weekdays by phone, chat, or text. Highly trained Victim Assistance Specialists provide emotional support and referrals to local resources. All referrals meet individual needs, and services are available in over 200 languages. Visit the Office of Victims and Crime at https://victimconnect.org.
>
> **National Association of Crime Victims Compensation Boards:** Victims and their families should apply for compensation in the state where the crime occurred. The Program Directory links each state's compensation program and provides specific information about benefits, requirements, and procedures. Visit the National Association of Crime Victims Compensation Boards at https://nac vcb.org/state-information.
>
> **988 Suicide and Crisis Lifeline:** The 988 Suicide and Crisis Lifeline offers 24/7 phone, text, and chat access to trained crisis counselors who can help people experiencing any mental health crisis. People can also call 988 if they are worried about a loved one who may need crisis support. Crisis counselors can also help link people in crisis

to community-based providers for ongoing services. Visit the 988 Suicide and Crisis Lifeline at https://988lifeline.org or dial the code 988. (**Note**: The previous Lifeline phone number (1-800-273-8255) will always remain available to people in emotional distress or suicidal crisis.)

National Domestic Violence Hotline: The National Domestic Violence Hotline offers 24/7 phone, text, and chat resources and support to survivors of intimate partner violence. They can help survivors create safety plans when attempting to leave violent relationships and provide local resources for help. Visit the National Domestic Violence Hotline at https://thehotline.org or call the hotline at 1-800-799-SAFE.

Ongoing Care: After Stabilization

Mental Health Therapy

Many survivors and their loved ones report that mental health therapy was essential to their recovery. Psychotherapy (referred to as "talk therapy") can reduce anxiety symptoms, strengthen coping skills, and help survivors work out their painful emotions. It helps decrease symptoms of hyperarousal that interfere with sleep, appetite, and physical healing. Psychotherapy can help survivors regain a sense of safety in the world and build hope.

But how does one access psychotherapy? There are many types of therapies, and it can be confusing for survivors to navigate the process of finding treatment, particularly during the crisis phase and soon after.

Various types of mental health treatment are available, and there are several titles for licensed therapists. All licensed mental health clinicians are highly trained professionals who can assess, diagnose, and treat various psychological conditions. The licenses commonly recognized in the United States are licensed clinical psychologists, licensed professional counselors, licensed marriage and family therapists, and licensed clinical social workers. Though therapists can provide treatment, they typically have different areas of interest and specialties. Not all therapists are skilled in trauma recovery work. Those with special education and training in treating trauma generally use the term "trauma-informed."

Therapists and clients work collaboratively, and the right match is essential. Survivors should choose a therapist who creates a sense of comfort. They need to feel understood. The therapist should explain the type of treatment they provide.

Though there are many techniques that trauma-informed therapists use, research has consistently shown that one variable—more than any other—is associated with treatment benefit: the quality of the relationship between the client and the therapist. This relationship is more important than any technique the therapist may provide.

Specific therapy techniques are tools in the toolkit. Mental health clinicians use various tools based on what works well for each individual. Trauma-informed therapists use multiple techniques since different tools benefit varying healing stages.

Following are some of the more common techniques used by trauma-informed mental health therapists:

- Eye Movement Desensitization and Reprocessing (EMDR) is a type of cognitive therapy that encourages the client to focus briefly on the trauma memory while simultaneously experiencing bilateral stimulation (typically eye movements). Many find this technique reduces the vividness and painful emotion associated with traumatic memories.
- Dialectical Behavioral Therapy (DBT) is talk therapy specially adapted for people who experience intense and painful emotions. DBT helps survivors understand their emotional reactions and learn how to manage complicated feelings.
- Somatic/Polyvagal Therapy focuses on helping clients access healing by tracking sensations in their bodies in the present moment and becoming more consciously aware of their inner experiences. The goal is to help clients feel calm and stable by working with physical sensations and gentle movements.
- Guided imagery includes a guided meditation to promote relaxation and ease the stress response. It helps clients gain skills in self-soothing and managing painful memories. A clinician can create therapeutic metaphors for their client's needs.
- Narrative therapy helps individuals express the stories of their lives and contextualize traumatic experiences. It can help provide clarity so that trauma symptoms become less overwhelming. It increases a sense of agency as the survivor learns to rewrite the story of their lives and create a positive future narrative.

There are multiple ways to find a trauma-informed therapist or psychiatrist, and here are just a few:

- Physicians or hospital social workers can offer referrals.
- Health insurance companies can provide members with a list of approved mental health clinicians filtered according to their specialties.
- Many communities have local Victim-Witness Assistance offices that maintain a list of trauma therapists.
- County behavioral health agencies generally have referral lists for low-income or uninsured people who need mental health support.
- *Psychology Today* offers a free search engine, "Find a therapist," which allows one to search by location and specialty at www.psychologytoday.com/us/therapists.

Try to speak with a therapist before scheduling an appointment, as most mental health clinicians offer a free initial phone consultation.

Psychopharmacology

Psychopharmacology is the scientific study of psychotropic medications and their impact on biology, particularly the nervous system, which is interwoven intimately with the body. Modern psychotropic medications are safe and nonaddictive; most work by modifying how neurotransmitters (chemical messengers) in the brain work. Neurotransmitters can become altered after major traumas or stressors contributing to PTSD symptoms. Several medications can be helpful to those in the crisis phase or with ongoing PTSD.

While psychotherapists provide talk therapy, psychiatrists and mental health nurse practitioners provide medication that helps with mental health conditions like PTSD. Many survivors and their loved ones have found that the combination of talk therapy with prescription medication has been most beneficial in their recovery.

Here is a brief description of psychiatrists and primary mental health nurse practitioners:

- Psychiatrists are medical doctors who have completed medical school and had additional specialized training in psychopharmacology.
- Primary mental health nurse practitioners are nurses with advanced training in psychopharmacology.

Any primary care physician can offer referrals to a psychiatrist or primary mental health nurse practitioner.

Complementary Healing Modalities

Many forms of additional self-help and supportive activities can be powerful and promote healing. However, these practices must be led by those who are trauma-informed. When directed by those who do not understand the unique needs of survivors, they can exacerbate symptoms of PTSD, including flashbacks and dissociation.

Trauma-informed approaches make the following practices more accessible and safer since they address the unique needs of survivors:

- Mindfulness Meditation is the practice of learning to sustain attention to the present moment, in essence, to be "mindful." Trauma memories interfere with this process by taking survivors into the past, where they re-experience fear and pain. Without guidance, those with PTSD can experience emotional dysregulation when beginning to meditate.

A trauma-informed meditation teacher knows how to work with trauma survivors to stay grounded in the present moment and maintain a state of emotional regulation through specific techniques involving breath, sensations, and sound.

- Trauma-informed, restorative yoga differs from traditional yoga and incorporates gentle, soothing movement and somatic awareness. Trauma doesn't just affect the mind—it affects the body. Trained trauma-informed yoga teachers understand how trauma in the body intersects with the yoga practice. It does not emphasize holding extreme physical poses or pushing through discomfort; it emphasizes body awareness and feelings of safety. It can help with nervous system dysregulation and feelings of disconnection from the body. The emphasis is on physical and emotional security.
- Peer support groups allow survivors to connect with others who have had similar experiences. Such groups reduce the sense of isolation survivors often feel and provide a safe place to share intensely painful emotions and memories. Survivors learn coping skills from other survivors.

The resources noted in this chapter are a source of valuable information for the reader. However, this is not a substitute for direct expert assistance. If such assistance is required, the services of a competent professional should be sought. A coordinated multidisciplinary approach between law enforcement, medical staff, and mental health care providers is compassionate and effective.

*Content disclaimer: Although the publisher and the editors have made every effort to ensure that the information in this book was correct at press time, and while this publication is designed to provide accurate information regarding the subject matter covered, the publisher and the editors assume no responsibility for errors, inaccuracies, omissions, or any other inconsistencies herein and hereby disclaim any liability to any party for any loss, damage, or disruption caused by errors or omissions, whether such errors or omissions result from negligence, accident or any other cause.

Index

physical therapy: Long, Margaret 6; Nowlan, Joshua 71; Richardson, Darien 18
Pierce, Jennifer L. 3
playing dead 16
pneumonia 7
police: Dayton, Ohio mass shooting (August 2019) 61; DelaVergne, Caia 15, 16; Gazzani, Vincent 76; Lasher-Sommers, Clai 40; Long, Margaret 12; Louisville, Kentucky mass shooting (May 2020) 50, 51; murders by 52; Neary, Kevin 24; Ranta, Kate 28–32, 34, 37–8; Route 91 Harvest festival mass shooting, Las Vegas (October 2017) 56; Stepakoff, Josh 45, 47
Polyvagal Therapy 86
post-traumatic stress disorder (PTSD) 27, 49, 83; alcohol use 53; Buhr, Alayna 63; Cantrell, Emily 69; complementary healing modalities 87; courtroom testimony 75; exposure and recovery 45; Lasher-Sommers, Clai 42, 43; Nowlan, Joshua 73; psychopharmacology 89; Ranta, Kate, and family 31, 32, 36, 37; Richardson, Darien 14, 19, 20; Van Velzer, Ryan 52, 54
poverty *see* financial stress
powerlessness 27, 32
primary mental health nurse practitioners 87
prison system: DelaVergne, Caia 16; Gazzani, Vincent 76; Lasher-Sommers, Clai 40; Long, Margaret 12; Ranta, Kate 32, 34, 36, 37, 40; Stepakoff, Josh 46
privacy, loss of 21
prosthetics: DelaVergne, Caia 16; Nowlan, Joshua 2, 71
protective orders 41; *see also* restraining orders
psychiatrists 87
Psychology Today 86
psychopathy 36
psychopharmacology 87
psychotherapy *see* therapy

quality of life 2

rage *see* anger and rage
random open fire 75–8

Ranta, Kate 27, 28, 30–40
Ranta, Robert 28–32, 33–7
Ranta, Susan 28, 37–40
Ranta, William 28–1, 32–9
religion 58–61
remembrance events 79, 80, *80*
reporters *see* news media
respiratory machine dependence 2
restraining orders 31–2
Richardson, Darien 14, 18–22
Richardson, Judi 15, 19–22
robbery, armed 23–6

sadness 59
safety, feelings of 83; Buhr, Alayna 61; DelaVergne, Caia 14; Richardson, Darien 19
San Diego shootings (April 2021) 76–8
scars, physical: DelaVergne, Caia *15*; Gazzani, Vincent 75, 76–8; insensitive questions about 75, 78; Korellis, Patrick 80–2; Long, Margaret *6*; Nowlan, Joshua 71, 73; Ranta, Kate 31, *33*
school shootings 79–82; fear of 63
Scott, Shavaun 2
sedation 25
shame 27
social media: activism 3; DelaVergne, Caia, shooter of 16; Louisville, Kentucky mass shooting (May 2020) 52; mass shooting victims Facebook group 80, 81
sociopathy 35
Somatic/Polyvagal Therapy 86
spinal injuries 24–5
spirituality 58–1
spousal abuse *see* domestic violence
States United to Prevent Gun Violence 42
Stepakoff, Josh 46–8
stress: Ranta, Robert and Susan 36, 37; *see also* post-traumatic stress disorder
stress response: DelaVergne, Caia 14; domestic violence 27; hate crime 45; Johnston, Alicia 53
support systems 5, 14, 27; DelaVergne, Caia 14; Lasher-Sommers, Clai 40; Long, Margaret 8–9, 10; Neary, Kevin 23, 24; peer support groups 88; resources 83–8; Richardson, Darien 14, 19–20; Stepakoff, Josh 47; *see also* caregiving; family and friends

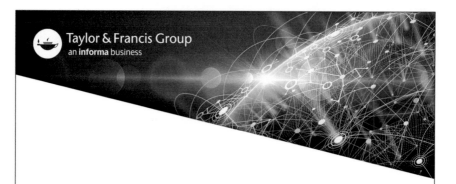